Basics
for
Bank Directors

Forest E. Myers

Commercially reprinted 2010
Originally published by
DIVISION OF SUPERVISION AND RISK MANAGEMENT
FEDERAL RESERVE BANK OF KANSAS CITY

Art and promotional copy (c) Booklife 2010
ISBN 978-1-105-81038-1

This is a commercial reprint

In recent years, alleged wrongdoing and prosecution of corporate officials at publicly traded firms have filled the press. News accounts highlight blatantly abusive practices on the part of these officials, causing many to ask what the board of directors was doing while management enriched itself at the expense of shareholders. After all, the board is ultimately responsible for ensuring the corporation is run for the benefit of its owners and other stakeholders and, in meeting its responsibilities, the board of directors oversees management of the business.

Banks are corporations, and their boards, like those of other corporations, are expected to exercise management oversight. Because of this, bank supervisors rely on directors as a first-line of defense for ensuring banks are run safely and are compliant with laws and regulations. Where oversight is strong, problems are addressed and corrected early. Where oversight is weak or nonexistent, problems remain uncorrected, possibly resulting in bank failure

Recognizing the key role directors play in well-run banks, the Federal Reserve Bank of Kansas City has, for more than a decade, offered *Basics for Bank Directors* as a resource for bank directors. The primary goal of this book is to provide directors, especially non-management directors who may have little knowledge about banks and their operation, with basic information to help them be intelligent questioners of risk taking and risk management at their institutions. In it, we share information gained from years of supervisory experience; information that we believe will help directors meet their oversight responsibilities. We offer ideas, matters to consider, and tools directors can use in guiding their banks.

As a further aid, the Federal Reserve System offers an online companion course, *Insights for Bank Directors*. This course focuses on bank financial analysis and the control of credit, liquidity, and market risks, permitting directors to apply the tools discussed in this book. There is no charge to use the course. It is available at (www.stlouisfed.org/col/director). We hope you find both useful.

THOMAS M. HOENIG
President

April, 2005

Acknowledgments

Once again, I am indebted to others who helped me in the update and production of this book. Without their expertise, support, and special effort, this book would not exist and be in your hands now. Special thanks to Andrew Thompson and Jeni McCormick for their content suggestions regarding the Bank Secrecy Act and the USA PATRIOT Act. Thanks also to Mark Schulte who offered suggestions to update the text regarding bank capital adequacy and to Jane Padget for her advice on bank accounting, audit, and operations risk management matters. Once again, I am indebted to Dave Klose, who continues to share his expertise on bank supervision and his talent as an editor, for the gift of his time and his content suggestions. Additionally, I thank Lori Hand for her editorial work and suggested improvements to the text, to Beth Norman for her layout and formatting of the text for publication, and to Casey McKinley for his update and redesign of the cover.

FOREST E. MYERS
Economist

Table of Contents

> *In today's world, commercial banks are fighting hard to maintain their historic role as leaders of the financial community. They are faced with increasing pressures from competitive institutions which are eager to offer services that have heretofore been restricted to banks;... A bank director, particularly a non-management director, has a greater opportunity and a greater responsibility today than at any period in recent history ...* [1]

These words were written 30 years ago. Yet, they have a familiar ring and could just as easily describe challenges facing banks and bank leadership today. If anything, events of the last three decades serve only to reinforce this earlier observation; banks must work harder to meet shareholder profit expectations, and more is expected from bank directors.

Since the 1970s, increased competition from other financial service providers, deregulation, financial and technological innovations, and economic swings have made it increasingly difficult for bank management to steer a consistently profitable course. As a result, a large number of banks have failed, and many more have merged or been acquired by others.

Additionally, legal changes and court actions have placed greater responsibility and accountability on bank directors. For example, the Financial Institutions Reform, Recovery and Enforcement Act of 1989 strengthened enforcement authority and increased penalties the federal regulatory agencies can assess against directors and others for problems at banks. The Federal Deposit Insurance Corporation Improvement Act of 1991 required board review of more matters and placed greater responsibility on outside directors in larger banking organizations. Subsequent court decisions have clarified tests of director negligence and made it easier for the Federal Deposit Insurance Corporation (FDIC) to pursue claims in some states against directors of failed institutions for which it is appointed receiver. More recently, the Sarbanes-Oxley Act of 2002, stock and other exchange listing requirements, and bank regulatory guidance

1

stressed greater independence of outside directors and generally raised expectations regarding their oversight of bank management.

As the future unfolds, outside directors will play an increasingly important role in guiding their banks and serving as unbiased judges of their operational performance.[2] Fulfilling this role will not be easy. Studies of failed banks reveal that many were supervised by directors who received insufficient or untimely information or who were inattentive to the bank's affairs. This impaired their ability to judge bank operations and to identify and correct problems. Thus, if outside directors are to meet the demands placed upon them, they must be more knowledgeable, better informed, and more active in identifying and correcting problems in their banks. In light of these challenges, some may ask "why serve as an outside bank director?" In response, banks play an important role in the economic lives of their communities, and many consider board service to be an honor. Although there may have been a variety of reasons (prominence in the community, knowledge of the community and its people, business expertise, etc.) why you were invited to serve as a director, your selection to the board is testimony to the valuable contribution the bank's shareholders believe you can provide to its management.

Additionally, the director's job may not be as daunting as it first appears. Basic management experience and skills necessary to succeed in other endeavors are equally applicable to banks. Thus, the knowledge and experience you have developed in other walks of life can be effectively used in looking after bank affairs. Add to this a questioning attitude and a willingness to commit time and energy to bank matters and you have many of the attributes of an effective bank director. The only thing that may be missing is a basic knowledge of banking and an awareness of specific matters to consider in overseeing a bank.

This booklet recognizes the special need for outside directors to build familiarity with banking. It provides basic information on banks and their supervision and suggests matters directors might want to pay close attention to in supervising their banks. Many approaches could be followed to accomplish this broad purpose. The approach used here employs many of the methods, techniques, and reports used by examiners to evaluate bank condition and compliance. This is not to suggest that you, as an outside director, should behave as a bank examiner nor is it meant to suggest that examiners should assume your role as an outside director. Rather, you, like the examiner, must be able to draw conclusions about your bank's condition in a relatively short time without intimate knowledge of its daily operations. An "examiner-like" approach lets you do this by focusing attention on key bank operations and giving you an organized way to "get up to speed" on bank affairs.

The discussion that follows does not offer "how-to" ideas on meeting all your duties and responsibilities as a bank director. There are many books and publications by bankers, consultants, academicians, regulatory agencies, and others that cover the waterfront of your directorship responsibilities. Instead, the focus is on a small but important aspect of your responsibilities—the part that deals with your bank's compliance with laws and regulations and its financial soundness. Chapter 1 addresses the first of these matters. It briefly sets out the purposes of regulation, discusses the role bank regulatory agencies play in achieving these purposes, and discusses your responsibility for regulatory compliance. Chapter 2 addresses matters pertaining to financial soundness. It discusses bank capital, asset quality, management, earnings, liquidity, and market risk sensitivity and presents ideas that you may find useful in monitoring these key bank performance areas. Chapter 3 suggests additional sources you may find useful in further building your knowledge of banking matters.

Endnotes

[1] Theodore Brown, "The Director and the Banking System," *The Bank Director*, ed. Richard B. Johnson, (Dallas: SMU Press, 1974), p. 3.

[2] Outside bank directors differ from "inside" or "management" directors in that they do not also serve as officers and management officials of the bank and own less than 5 percent of its stock.

Chapter 1

REGULATORY COMPLIANCE

L aws and regulations govern many aspects of banking. Matters such as who owns, controls, and manages banks; how much banks can lend to a single customer or group of customers; how much capital banks should have; where banks can locate their offices; and what services banks can provide are all addressed by banking laws and regulations.

As a director, you are responsible for establishing policies and monitoring operations to ensure your bank complies with laws and regulations. To fulfill this responsibility, you must have a basic understanding of the regulatory framework under which your bank operates and be knowledgeable about the rules and regulations to which it must adhere.

The discussion that follows helps build this knowledge. It reviews the broad purposes of regulation and outlines the basic responsibilities of the banking agencies to achieve these purposes. Additionally, it presents laws and regulations that may be of particular interest to directors and provides a summary of compliance pitfalls often associated with them.

Banking Supervision and Regulation

The laws and regulations that govern banking have evolved over the years and have come to be thought of as accomplishing several broad purposes. These purposes include maintaining or promoting:

- A safe, sound, and stable banking system.

- An efficient and competitive banking system.

- An "even-handed" or "fair" banking system.[1]

A stable banking system

The promotion of a safe, sound, and stable banking system is one of the most basic reasons for bank supervision and regulation. A stable banking system provides depositors with a secure place to keep their funds. It provides businesses and individuals a dependable framework for conducting monetary transactions. Finally, it provides the Federal Reserve a reliable channel through which to conduct monetary policy.

Deposit insurance and the Federal Reserve System's discount window are two important tools for achieving banking stability.[2] Together, they are a significant part of the federal safety net for banking, providing depositors protection against loss of funds up to insurance limits and giving solvent banks access to liquidity when the need arises.[3] By doing so, they reduce the probability of systemic bank runs and panics.

To help reduce calls on the federal safety net, government uses a system of bank regulation and supervision. Regulations place limits or prohibit practices that experience indicates may cause banking problems.[4] Supervision includes on-site examinations which are used to determine a bank's compliance with regulations, the effectiveness of its control systems, and the state of its financial condition. Supervision also includes off-site monitoring of a bank's financial trends and other actions bank regulators take to correct troubles at problem banks.

Agencies at both the federal and state levels are responsible for regulating and supervising banks. A bank's charter class and whether or not the bank is a member of the Federal Reserve System determine the agencies that supervise it. Banks chartered by the federal government are national banks, and their primary supervisor is the Office of the Comptroller of the Currency (OCC). Banks chartered by the states are state banks. These banks are supervised by their chartering authority and the FDIC or the Federal Reserve System. Banks that elect Federal Reserve membership are referred to as "state member banks," and their federal banking supervisor is the Federal Reserve System.[5] State banks that do not elect Federal Reserve membership are "state nonmember banks," and their federal supervisor is the FDIC.

A bank's primary supervisor administers the safety and soundness regulations under which it operates. This supervisor also conducts periodic examinations of the bank (see Box 1.1). For national banks, the OCC does the examinations. For state banks, the state banking agencies, along with the Federal Reserve or FDIC, conduct them. To avoid duplication of effort and to reduce cost, state agencies may rotate examination responsibilities or conduct joint examinations with the appropriate federal agency.

Box 1.1

BANK EXAMINATIONS

Bank examinations are an important supervisory tool. The agencies use examinations to periodically assess the overall condition of an institution, its risk exposures, and its compliance with laws and regulations. Depending upon circumstances, your bank is examined every 12 to 18 months.*

Over the years, the agencies have worked to make the examination process more effective, to ease examination burdens on banks, to make examinations more consistent among agencies, and to improve communication of examination findings. Most recently, they altered the examination process in order to respond to rapid changes occurring at financial institutions. For example, it wasn't too long ago that examiners arrived unannounced at a bank to determine its financial condition and regulatory compliance by laboriously going through its books and records. This quote by a bank examiner provides a good perspective on examination process that continued until not long ago.

My first assignment in June 1971 was to participate in the examination of the largest bank in the...District. The surprise examination started on Friday after banking hours. It included our examination staff plus people from the auditing and securities areas of the [Reserve] Bank. We gathered en masse in front of the [Reserve] Bank and marched down the hill to Commerce Bank and Trust. There we spent Friday night and Saturday counting cash and securities and proving the bank's ledgers. **

Continued on following page

Box 1.1 *(continued)*

Today, bank examiners still arrive en masse at a bank. However, examinations are generally announced in advance, and the process used to determine an institution's financial health focuses more on the institution's risk exposures and its risk control systems than checking on its balance sheet values. This new examination approach focuses on management processes and often is referred to as "risk-focused" or "supervision-by-risk." The older approach, with its emphasis on verification, is often referred to as a "transactions approach" to bank examination.

Examiners have always been interested in the integrity and quality of a bank's control systems. However, with the rapid change in financial products and activities conducted by institutions, these systems are more critical to their safe and sound operation. As a result, internal control systems receive even greater examiner attention. This increased emphasis on controls provides the supervisory agencies with a better picture of an institution's ability to effectively deal with future events and to successfully enter new activities.

Under the risk-focused examination approach, the banking agencies (federal and state) customize their examinations to suit the size and complexity of an institution and to concentrate examination resources on activities that may pose significant risk (for example, credit, liquidity, market, operational, legal, and reputational risks) to it. Off-site, prior to an examination, examiners determine the institution's significant activities and the types and amount of risk exposure these activities pose. During this risk assessment process, they review previous examination reports and current financial data. Many times they conduct telephone interviews or they make a pre-examination visit to the bank. At this time, examiners discuss with the bank's senior management matters such as the bank's economic and competitive environment; recent or contemplated changes in personnel, procedures, operations, and organization; internal audit, monitoring, and compliance programs; and management's own assessment of the

Box 1.1 *(continued)*

bank's risk areas. Additionally, they review internal policies and procedures, management reports, internal and external audit reports, audit report work papers, strategic plans and budgets, minutes of board of directors and committee meetings, and other materials necessary to gain insights regarding the extent and reliability of the bank's internal risk management systems. In the process of doing this, examiners form an initial assessment of the bank's management. Also at this time, they ask for basic information on individual loans in the bank's portfolio—for example, original loan amount, current loan balance, borrower name, payment history, etc. Later, an initial review of capital adequacy, earnings, liquidity, and market risk is completed and questions to be asked on-site are identified. Also, loans to be reviewed are determined. This loan sample often includes: all loan relationships—including loan commitments—above a certain dollar size (the loan cut), all loans past due 30 days or more or on nonaccrual status, all previously classified loans, all loans to insiders, all loans on the bank's watch or problem loan list, and a random sample of loans from the remainder of the loan portfolio with balances below the loan cut. Once this preliminary work is completed, the information is used to develop a strategy for directing examination resources to significant, high-risk areas of the bank's operations.

On-site, examiners review high-risk areas (for example, review loans and investments, analyze internal loan quality grades, compare daily practice against policy/procedure requirements). They also continue their assessment of the bank's risk management systems and their evaluation of the institution's management.

When on-site work is completed, examiners hold an exit meeting with senior management to discuss preliminary examination results. Matters discussed at this meeting may vary. However, topics often covered include the scope of examination, condition of the bank (a review of the CAMELS components and composite rating), and the

Continued on following page

Box 1.1 *(continued)*

quality of management oversight and processes. As part of the bank's management team, you may want to attend the exit meeting because it provides you with an advanced look at any strengths or weaknesses identified by the examiners. In some instances, such as in the case of a troubled bank, examiners may ask you to attend.

Subsequent to on-site work, examiners prepare their examination report. After the report is completed, it is forwarded to the institution's board of directors and senior management. Like reports done in the past, the examination report provides a rating for the institution's capital, asset quality, management, earnings, liquidity, and sensitivity to market risk. It points out operational and control system strengths and weaknesses in each of these areas. Because examination reports represent a "third-party" assessment of your institution's risk-taking, the quality of its risk management, and its regulatory compliance, it is a valuable tool in helping you exercise effective oversight over many aspects of your bank.

---

*State guidelines on examination frequency vary. However, Section 10(d) of the Federal Deposit Insurance Act, as amended, requires that every bank and savings and loan receive a "full-scope," on-site examination every 12 months. However, this may be extended to 18 months if an institution: (1) has total assets of less than $250 million; (2) is well capitalized; (3) is well managed; (4) is composite rated 1 or 2 at its most recent examination; (5) is not subject to a formal enforcement proceeding or order; and (6) has not undergone a change in control during the previous 12 months.

**Presentation by John E. Yorke, senior vice president, December 12, 1996, to the Board of Directors, Federal Reserve Bank of Kansas City.

Many times, banks are owned and controlled by other corporations, bank holding companies (BHCs). Originally formed to avoid location and product restrictions on banks and later to provide bank owners certain tax advantages, BHCs are an important feature of the nation's banking system, controlling around 95 percent of U.S. banking assets at year-end 2004. A more recent addition to our financial system is the financial holding company (FHC). These companies, authorized by the Gramm-Leach-Bliley Act of 1999 (GLB), are bank holding companies that can engage in financial or financially related activities not otherwise permitted for bank holding companies.[6] The Federal Reserve System exercises consolidated supervisory oversight of BHCs and FHCs, meaning that it is the "umbrella supervisor" for these companies. Functional regulators, however, retain supervisory responsibility for the portions of BHCs and FHCs that fall within their jurisdiction. For example, OCC supervises national bank subsidiaries, FDIC and state banking agencies supervise state nonmember bank subsidiaries, state insurance commissioners supervise insurance subsidiaries, and the Securities and Exchange Commission supervises broker/dealer subsidiaries.

A competitive banking system

Another important purpose of bank regulation is the maintenance of a competitive banking system. A competitive banking system provides customers with the lowest priced, most efficiently produced goods and services.

A number of laws and regulations influence banking competition. Chartering and branching laws and regulations establish minimum standards for opening new banks and bank branch offices and thereby influence banking competition. Additionally, other banking statutes (the Bank Merger Act, the Change in Bank Control Act, and the Bank Holding Company Act) prohibit merger and acquisition transactions that create or tend to create a monopoly in any part of the country. Banking law (the Management Interlocks Act) also prohibits management interlocks among unaffiliated institutions located in the same community in order to reduce possible anti-competitive behavior.

Both state and federal banking agencies play a role in maintaining an efficient and competitive banking system. For example, the OCC and state agencies have responsibility for chartering new banks. The three federal banking agencies and state banking agencies are responsible for approving new branch offices. In addition, the federal banking agencies, through their applications processes, take primary responsibility for scrutinizing bank ownership and control changes, and bank mergers and acquisitions for their effects on banking competition.[7] The OCC performs this antitrust review on transactions involving national banks. The Federal Reserve and the FDIC perform similar reviews for transactions involving state member and nonmember

11

banks, respectively. The Federal Reserve does this review for transactions involving bank holding companies. The federal banking agencies also take primary responsibility for reviewing and determining the permissibility of director interlocks.

A fair banking system

Another important goal of regulation is consumer protection. Some laws, such as the Truth in Lending Act and the Truth in Savings Act, require banks to disclose information that helps consumers evaluate product options open to them. Other laws (for example, the Equal Credit Opportunity Act and the Community Reinvestment Act) require banks to be even-handed in their customer dealings. Additional laws (for example, the Fair Credit Reporting Act, the Fair Debt Collection Practices Act, GLB, and Fair and Accurate Credit Transaction Act) provide consumer safeguards in the extension, collection, and reporting of consumer credit and set out administrative, technical, and physical safeguards for customer records and information, including sharing of customer information.

Historically, Congress has looked to the Federal Reserve to draft federal consumer protection regulations. Individual state and federal banking agencies, however, have responsibility for supervising their constituent banks' compliance with these regulations.

The Director's Responsibility for Regulatory Compliance

Although you, as a bank director, are ultimately responsible for your bank's compliance with all applicable laws and regulations, certain of these deserve special mention because they specifically apply to directors or they present compliance issues that may frequently require your attention. These laws and regulations and a summary of their intended purposes are included in Table 1.1. Additionally, compliance pitfalls that are often encountered with each are mentioned to help you pinpoint potential trouble spots. Because of their importance, you should have some familiarity with these laws and regulations as well as any rulings your bank's primary supervisor may have issued on them.

Table 1.1

Laws and Regulations of Particular Interest to Directors

Law/Regulation	Compliance Reminders
The Bank Secrecy Act/Anti-Money Laundering (BSA/AML) (31 CFR 103) Keeps financial institutions from being used as intermediaries for criminal activities, or being used to hide the transfer of money derived from those activities. Also, sets out record keeping requirements in order to provide a "paper trail" that law enforcement can use, if necessary.	Make certain the bank has a program to ensure and monitor compliance with BSA reporting and record keeping requirements. The basic elements of the program must include internal controls to confirm program compliance, a designated individual responsible for coordinating day-to-day compliance, training for appropriate personnel, and periodic independent testing for BSA compliance. The BSA program must be in writing and approved by the board of directors, with the approval noted in board minutes. Also, the board should review the program at least annually and record the review and approval of the program in the minutes. Remember, management must notify the board anytime a Suspicious Activity Report ("SAR") is filed in accordance with the regulation implementing the BSA. Additionally, don't forget to have periodic (every 12 months is best, but no more than every 15 months) independent tests or reviews done to check the bank's BSA compliance. Bank personnel (as long as they are independent of the BSA compliance function) or an outside party can perform these tests. Currency Transaction Reports (CTRs) must be filed for each deposit, withdrawal, exchange of currency, or payment or transfer which involves a transaction in currency of more than $10,000. Multiple transactions must be treated as a single transaction if the institution knows that *Continued on following page*

Law/Regulation	Compliance Reminders
The Bank Secrecy Act/Anti-Money Laundering (BSA/AML) (31 CFR 103) *(Continued)*	(1) the transactions are by or on behalf of the same person, and (2) they result in either cash received or currency disbursed by the institutions totaling more than $10,000 during any one business day. If a transaction is suspicious and above $10,000, a CTR and a SAR must be filed. Remember, a CTR must be filed within 15 calendar days, 25 days if filed electronically, of the transaction being reported. Copies of CTRs must be held for five years from the date filed. Institutions can file to designate certain customers as an "exempt person" under the currency transaction reporting rules. There are two categories of exemptions: Phase I, which are referred to as listed businesses, and Phase II, which consist primarily of non-listed businesses. "Listed businesses" include a bank's domestic operations, agencies or departments of federal, state, or local governments, and any entity whose common stock or analogous equity is listed on any stock exchange. "Non-listed businesses" consist of commercial enterprises which have maintained a transaction account at the bank for at least 12 months, engage in at least eight currency transactions a year that require reporting, and are incorporated and/or registered in the U.S. Phase I exemption forms only have to be filed once, while Phase II exemptions must be reviewed annually for continued eligibility and renewed every two years by March 15 after the initial exemption filing. Documentation providing the basis for exemption from CTR filing requirements must be retained for five years. Remember, exempting a customer does not relieve the bank of its responsibility to monitor the customer for suspicious activity.

Law/Regulation	Compliance Reminders
USA PATRIOT Act (ACT) (31 CFR 103) Among other things, the ACT amends the Bank Secrecy Act to enhance prevention, detection, and prosecution of money laundering and terrorism by requiring financial institutions to verify the identity of new customers. The ACT also includes provisions to enhance sharing of customer information among financial institutions, law enforcement agencies, and the federal government.	Make certain the bank has the necessary customer identification programs to ensure it knows the identity of its new customers. These programs should collect identification information at account opening, provide for verifying new customer information, document information used to verify customer information, and provide for comparing new customers' names against government lists of known and suspected terrorist organizations. Additionally, ensure the bank has a process for documenting searches of financial records for information pertaining to individuals who are subjects of federal law enforcement investigations involving terrorism and/or money laundering and its response to those requesting information.
Federal Reserve Regulation L (12 CFR 212) Prohibits management interlocks among unaffiliated institutions in the same community.	Be aware of limits on your service as a director or management official at other unaffiliated banks, savings and loans, credit unions, savings and loan holding companies, or bank holding companies. Be especially sensitive to multiple service if: your bank is large in size; any office of your bank is located within the same large metropolitan area as the other institution or one of its offices; or any office of your bank is located within 10 miles of an office of the other institution.

Law/Regulation	Compliance Reminders
Federal Reserve Regulation O (12 CFR 215) Limits loans to bank officers, directors, management officials, and principal shareholders ("insiders").	Remember to combine credit extensions to insiders with those of their immediate family and businesses to make sure that loans to insiders, individually and in aggregate, stay within lending limits specified in the regulation. Also, remember there is a limit on loans to a single insider and an aggregate limit on total loans to all insiders. Pay special attention to treatment given to insider overdrafts. They are extensions of credit and are specifically addressed by the Regulation. Be alert to loan transactions where insiders may directly or indirectly receive some benefit from loans being made. Be mindful that an insider's endorsement, or guarantee, can be considered an indirect extension of credit. Make sure extensions of credit by other banks to executive officers and principal shareholders of your bank are reported promptly.
Federal Reserve Regulation P (12 CFR 216) Governs treatment of consumer, nonpublic, personal information by financial institutions. Requires institutions to provide customers with a notice of their privacy policies and practices. Prohibits institutions from sharing nonpublic, consumer/customer financial information with nonaffiliated third parties unless the institutions meet certain disclosure and opt-out requirements and the consumer/customer hasn't opted out of the disclosure.	Remember the regulation requires an annual notice to customers. Also, make sure the bank's policies regarding its information sharing are consistent with its current sharing practices. Be particularly mindful of joint marketing agreements, their influences on sharing practices and content of notices to customers, and their compliance with consumer/customer opt-out election. Additionally, monitor consumer/customer opt-out to ensure the bank's processes are in compliance with its policies regarding sharing of nonpublic, personal customer information.

Law/Regulation	Compliance Reminders
Federal Reserve Regulation W (12 CFR 223) Limits transactions and loans between banks and affiliated companies. Requires transactions be on an arms-length basis.	Be alert to asset purchases from the parent bank holding company or its affiliates. Be sensitive to the quality of those assets and the terms of purchase. Your bank cannot buy a "low-quality" asset from an affiliate except under very limited circumstances. Be alert to parent bank holding company expenses and overdrafts paid by the bank. Also, be alert to taxes paid by the bank when its operating results are consolidated with those of the parent bank holding company. Be sure the bank receives its share of refunds and benefits from joint tax filings. In addition, be sensitive to timing of tax payments to the parent company. These payments should not be made too much in advance of when they are due or they may be considered a loan to the parent company. Be alert to transactions between the bank and firms controlled by insiders to make sure their terms are no less favorable than terms the bank would receive on similar transactions with an outsider. In this regard, be especially aware of management fees paid by the bank to its parent bank holding company. Be mindful of services received, their quality, and their cost. Use equal care with asset purchases, rental agreements, and lease contracts between the bank and firms owned by insiders to make sure they are on equivalent terms to those with outsiders.
Federal Reserve Regulation BB (12 CFR 228) Establishes a framework and sets out criteria by which a bank's federal banking supervisor assesses its record of meeting community credit needs and provides for taking this record into account in certain applications involving the bank.	Remember that the bank's most recent Community Reinvestment Act (CRA) rating is public information and must be made available to the public upon request. Be aware the assessment area set out by the bank is key to the evaluation of its record of helping meet community credit needs. Make sure the assessment area includes whole geographic areas, does not illegally discriminate, and does not arbitrarily exclude low- or moderate-income areas. Remember it is a good practice to periodically review the bank's assessment area to make sure it includes all the bank's branches, deposit-taking ATMs, and a substantial portion of its loans.

Law/Regulation	Compliance Reminders
Financial Institutions Reform, Recovery, and Enforcement Act Notices (12 U.S.C. 1831i(a)) Requires, in certain instances, prior notice of board changes and employment of senior officers or changes in senior officer responsibilities.	Remember that 30-day prior notice is required for any changes to the board of directors, employment of new senior officers, or changes in senior officer responsibilities if your bank is in troubled condition, is not in compliance with minimum capital requirements, or is required to do so by its federal banking supervisor. Be sensitive to contemplated stock transactions, such as treasury stock redemptions, that may take your ownership over 10 percent of the outstanding shares of the bank or its parent bank holding company because they may require a change in control notification. Also, prior notification is required, unless otherwise grandfathered under the Regulation, if a share purchase or actions by others would take your ownership to 25 percent or more of the bank's or its parent bank holding company's voting shares. Note also that a transaction that takes your ownership over 10 percent of any voting class of stock, and no one else has greater ownership, may require filing a notification. Additionally, be aware your ownership may be combined with others, as indicated in the Regulation (for example, immediate family members), in determining the need for a notification. Be sensitive to transactions where you place 10 percent or more of your bank's or its parent bank holding company's stock in a trust. Also, be sensitive to terms of shareholder agreements. Trusts and agreements may raise control or company issues and require filings under the Change in Bank Control Act or the Bank Holding Company Act, respectively. If the bank or its bank holding company is being sold, be mindful of terms of purchase options that may be used in their purchase. Options may give buyers control of the bank or company and require prior notification.

Law/Regulation	Compliance Reminders
Lending Limits Promotes diversification in a bank's loan portfolio by limiting loans to a single, non-insider borrower. The general lending limit to a single borrower for national banks is 15 percent of their capital and surplus plus an additional 10 percent of capital and surplus if the loan is fully secured by readily marketable collateral. Limits for state banks vary, depending upon the state of charter. Often, they are set from 15 to 30 percent of a bank's capital and surplus. State banking statutes should be consulted for specific lending limit information and for the method of calculating the limit. It is important to note that banks often establish an internal or "in-house" lending limit to further diversify their credit risk. The level at which the board of directors sets the internal limit depends upon its risk tolerance. At many banks, the board sets the in-house limit at 50 percent or less of the bank's legal lending limit.	Be cognizant of the bank's statutory lending limit and its internal lending limits. Loans and investments that approach these limits represent significant exposure of the bank's capital and should receive close scrutiny.
Safeguarding Customer Information (12 CFR 208.3(d)(1)) Requires banks to implement a comprehensive written information security program that ensures the security and confidentiality of customer information; protects the security and integrity of this information; and provides safeguards against its unauthorized access or use. The information security program is to identify internal and external risks associated with information technology systems and activities, ensure the implementation of risk mitigating controls, and establish periodic tests of key controls, systems, and procedures.	Remember to periodically test the key controls set out in the bank's information security program. Also remember that existing supervisory guidance on controlling information security risks extends to third-party service providers. Ongoing management and monitoring of the risks within such business relationships is a required part of an adequate customer information, safekeeping program.

In summary, banks operate under many laws, rules, and regulations. Your duty as a director requires that you establish policies to ensure regulatory compliance and to monitor the bank to make sure these policies are followed. Failure to perform this duty could expose your bank to loss and supervisory sanctions and you to a wide range of charges and penalties.[8]

Endnotes

[1]Kenneth R. Spong, Banking *Regulation: Its Purposes, Implementation, and Effects,* Fifth Edition (Kansas City: Federal Reserve Bank of Kansas City, 2000), pp. 5-10.

[2]The Federal Reserve discount window is a credit source that provides borrowing banks time to make orderly adjustments in their assets and/or liabilities to meet liquidity needs. Since January 2003, the discount window offers three credit programs—primary, secondary, and seasonal credit.

- Under the primary credit program, healthy institutions can borrow to meet short-term liquidity needs. To qualify for the program, an institution must be at least "adequately capitalized" under the federal banking agencies' capital guidelines and have a CAMELS composite rating of 3 or better. The interest rate charged for primary credit is currently 100 bps above the targeted federal funds rate.

- For those institutions that do not qualify for primary credit, secondary credit is available. Secondary credit also can be obtained to facilitate an orderly resolution of a troubled institution. Among other things, discount window staff reviews requests under this program to ensure that a borrowing institution can return to market funding. The rate for secondary credit program is 50 bps higher than that of the primary credit program.

- The seasonal credit program is available for longer periods (generally up to nine months) to assist smaller institutions in meeting regular funding needs arising from expected movement in their deposits and loans. The interest charged for seasonal credit is set by a formula tied to short-term market rates.

[3]The federal safety net for depository institutions is thought to include deposit insurance, access to the Federal Reserve's discount window and payment system guarantees, and the implicit certification of soundness that counterparties believe accompanies federal supervision and regulation. See Remarks by Governor Laurence H. Meyer at the 37th Annual Conference on Bank Structure and Competition of the Federal Reserve Bank of Chicago, Chicago, Illinois, May 10, 2001.

[4]For example, the General Accounting Office noted that bank regulators cited several factors as contributing to bank failure. These included inadequate or imprudent loan policies and procedures, poor credit analysis, weak loan administration, and poor loan documentation; inadequate supervision by the board of directors; heavy reliance on volatile funding sources; failure to establish an adequate loan loss reserve; and the presence of a dominant figure. Other factors noted were insider abuse and fraud. See *Bank Failures—Independent Audit Needed to Strengthen Internal Controls and Bank Management, AFMD-89-25*, (Washington, D.C.: United States General Accounting Office, May 1989) pp. 3-4.

[5]State chartered banks have the option of becoming Federal Reserve members. Federal Reserve membership is not optional for national banks.

[6]GLB also created financial subsidiaries for national banks that can engage in financial or financially related activities not otherwise permitted the bank. The powers granted these subsidiaries, however, are somewhat more limited than those given to FHCs. For example, financial subsidiaries may not engage in insurance underwriting, provide or issue annuities, or engage in merchant banking activities. FHCs may do so.

[7]See *Understanding Antitrust Considerations in Banking Proposals*, (Kansas City: Federal Reserve Bank of Kansas City, 1992) for a more detailed discussion of the review of banking transactions for their competitive effects.

[8]See *FDIC Manual of Examination Polices, Section 4.1 Management/Administration(http://www.fdic.gov/regulations/safety/manual/Section4-1_TOC. html)* for a basic discussion on bank director liability. Also, for a more general discussion on actions that the federal banking agencies may take against banks and their directors, see Robert E. Barnett, *Responsibilities and Liabilities of Bank and Bank Holding Company Directors, 4th ed.* (Chicago: Commerce Clearing House, Inc., 1996), pp. 51-65. Also, see Appendix C for details of allegations in FDIC suits against directors.

Chapter 2

BANK SOUNDNESS

In addition to compliance matters, you and other board members must be mindful of your bank's financial condition. This requires that you establish policies to establish your bank's risk limits, to govern its operations, and to safeguard its assets. It also requires that you periodically check bank performance to ensure policies are being followed and are achieving desired results.

The information to do this "checkup" can be obtained from internal reviews, directors' audits, external audits, examination reports, operating budgets, and the bank's financial reports. These sources can be used to judge the effectiveness of internal controls, to identify weaknesses where controls need to be strengthened or where additional controls may be needed, and to judge the bank's financial soundness.

There are many ways to organize the assessment of your bank's control systems and its financial condition. As suggested in the introduction to this booklet, one useful approach is to organize your soundness review around the outline used by the banking agencies. Under the Uniform Financial Institutions Rating System, the regulatory agencies evaluate and rate a bank's financial condition, operational controls, and compliance in six areas. These areas are **C**apital, **A**sset quality, **M**anagement, **E**arnings, **L**iquidity, and **S**ensitivity to market risk.[1] Each of these components is viewed separately and together to provide a summary picture of a bank's financial soundness, for example, its **CAMELS** rating. (See Box 2.1)

This chapter uses the CAMELS components as an outline for discussing matters relating to a bank's condition. It discusses the importance of each component, reviews topics that often are considered in evaluating them, and offers ideas on how each component can be evaluated. The first topic covered is bank capital. Subsequent sections deal with asset quality, management, earnings, liquidity, and market risk sensitivity.

Box 2.1

UNIFORM FINANCIAL INSTITUTION RATING SYSTEM (UFIRS)

The federal banking agencies (Agencies), adopted the UFIRS on November 13, 1979. An important reason for adopting this system was to provide the Agencies with a comprehensive and uniform way to evaluate an institution's soundness and to identify institutions that require special attention.

Originally, the UFIRS assessed a financial institution soundness in five areas—**C**apital, **A**sset quality, **M**anagement, **E**arnings, and **L**iquidity. However, starting in 1997, the Agencies added a sixth component to assess an institution's ability to monitor and manage market risk, the "**S**" or **S**ensitivity to market risk component.* Many times you may hear UFIRS referred to as the CAMELS rating system, an acronym for each of the six areas under which a financial institution is rated.

Under UFIRS, an institution receives a numeric score for each CAMELS component. It also receives a composite rating score that takes into account the individual CAMELS ratings and any other factors that in the opinion of the examiner may impinge on the financial institution's overall soundness.

The composite and component scores can take values ranging from 1 to 5. The best rating an institution can receive is a "1." A "1" rating indicates the strongest performance and risk management practices and the least supervisory concerns. A "5" is the worst rating an institution can receive. It indicates the weakest performance and inadequate risk management and raises the greatest level of supervisory concerns.

In the rating continuum, composite and component scores of "3" or higher are considered unsatisfactory. Additionally, as ratings go from 3 to 5, the level of supervisory concern increases, the ability of management to correct problems becomes less certain, the intrusion of supervisors becomes more pronounced, and the danger of failure

Box 2.1 *(continued)*

becomes more imminent. For example, an institution with a "3" composite rating is viewed as exhibiting some degree of supervisory concern in one or more component areas. "… Management may lack the ability or willingness to effectively address weaknesses within appropriate time frames. … require more than normal supervision, which may include formal or informal enforcement actions." A composite "4" rated institution is viewed as generally exhibiting "unsafe and unsound practices or conditions. There are severe financial or managerial deficiencies … weaknesses and problems are not being addressed or resolved by the board of directors and management … Close supervision is required … Failure is a distinct possibility if problems and weaknesses are not satisfactorily addressed or resolved." A composite "5" rated institution is viewed as exhibiting "extremely unsafe and unsound practices and conditions; … The volume and severity of problems are beyond management's ability or willingness to control or correct … Ongoing supervision is necessary … poses a significant risk to the deposit insurance fund and failure is highly probable."**

Since the late 1980s, the Agencies have provided directors and senior management with their bank's composite rating. Beginning January 1, 1997, the Agencies started providing the individual component ratings to directors and senior management.*** These actions were taken to help banks' management better understand supervisory issues, problems, and concerns with their institutions.

It is important to note that these ratings are intended for use by the bank's directors and senior management and are not to be disclosed to others.

*Federal Reserve System SR- 96-38 (Sup), Uniform Financial Rating System, December 27, 1996.

**Federal Reserve System SR 96-38 (Sup). In addition to adding the sixth component in 1996, the Agencies also modified the descriptions accompanying each component to emphasize in the rating management's ability to identify, measure, monitor, and control risks.

***Federal Reserve System, SR 96-26 (Sup), "Provision of Individual Components of Supervisory Rating System to Management and Boards of Directors," November 15, 1996.

CAPITAL

Bank capital serves the same purposes as capital in any other business. It is the cushion that protects a bank against unanticipated losses and sustains it through poor economic times. Likewise, bank capital is the pocket of funds that gives creditors comfort that their debts will be repaid. Since capital represents the shareholders' investment and appreciation in that investment from successful operations, it is also the shareholders' "stake put at risk," lessening incentives for taking unwarranted or uncompensated chances in operating the bank.

Different industries have varying needs for capital. Relative to nonfinancial businesses, banks and other financial service providers operate with small amounts of capital. Today, the average equity capital-to-asset ratio for banks hovers near 9.1 percent (Chart 2.1).

Chart 2.1

CAPITAL-TO-ASSET COMPARISON
BANKING AND OTHER INDUSTRY GROUPS

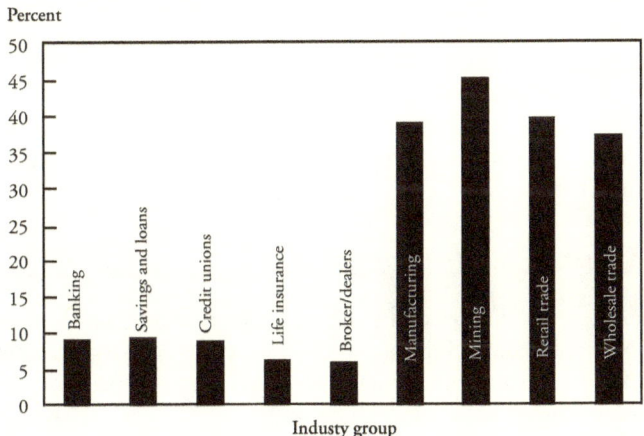

Percent

Industy group

Note: All data are for year-end 2003 or early 2004.

Source: Regulatory filings, Board of Governors, *Flow of Funds*, January 2004; U.S. Department of Commerce, *Quarterly Financial Reports*, December 2003

Many businesses with such little capital support would find it difficult to borrow funds to support their operations. Yet, banks experience little difficulty obtaining the deposits they need to fund their operation, and when they do, it is generally at lower rates than those available to other borrowers. The principal reason for this is the protection afforded bank depositors by federal deposit insurance. This protection in effect makes the federal government a cosigner on the insured portion of bank deposit liabilities, enabling banks to operate with far less capital than other firms.

Although federal deposit insurance protects depositors, a bank's thin capital provides little room for error. A sudden, unexpected interest rate change, losses on loans and investments, lawsuits, or embezzlement may leave a bank with inadequate capital protection and in some instances push it into insolvency. Because of this, the adequacy of a bank's capital position is an important concern for both bankers and bank regulators.

As a bank director, you are responsible for making sure your bank's capital is adequate for safe and sound operation. Fulfilling this responsibility entails monitoring and evaluating your bank's capital position and planning for its capital needs.

This section discusses capital adequacy. It describes regulatory guidelines for bank capital, addresses how capital is measured, discusses the need for bank capital planning, and offers ways to judge a bank's capital position.

Bank Capital and Its Regulation

Regulatory guidelines define capital and spell out the minimum acceptable capital levels for banks. The purpose of these guidelines is to increase depositor protection and to reduce deposit insurance fund losses.[2] Currently, the three federal banking agencies use a "risk-based" approach to gauge bank capital. Under this approach, the agencies define what is to be included in bank capital and establish the minimum capital a bank must have to protect it, primarily from the inherent risk in its asset holdings.

Risk-based capital guidelines divide capital into core and supplemental capital. Core or Tier 1 capital is similar to what is normally thought of as capital in other businesses. It consists of common and certain preferred stock, surplus, and undivided profits. Supplemental or Tier 2 capital consists, within certain specified limits, of such things as the allowance for loan losses, hybrid capital instruments, and subordinated debt. These supplemental items are often forms of debt that are subordinate to claims of depositors and the FDIC. As such, they provide depositor protection and are included in bank capital.

The sum of Tier 1 and Tier 2 capital, less certain deductions, represents a bank's total capital. In the capital guidelines, Tier 1 capital must constitute at least 50 percent of a bank's total capital. Thus, the use of Tier 2 capital is limited by the "hard" equity in a bank's capital structure. Table 2.1 provides a summary of the components that make up core and supplemental capital and indicates limitations on their use. Specific definitions for items in the table can be found in the capital guidelines published by the federal banking agencies.

As part of their capital adequacy assessment, the regulatory agencies convert a bank's assets, including off-balance sheet items, to risk equivalent assets.[3] The purpose of this conversion is to quantify the relative risk, primarily credit risk, in these assets and to determine the minimum capital necessary to compensate for this risk. For example, assets that pose little risk, such as cash held at the bank's offices and U.S. government securities, are weighted zero, meaning that no capital support is required for these assets. Assets that pose greater risk are weighted at 20, 50, or 100 percent of their dollar value, indicating the level of capital support they require. For illustrative purposes, Table 2.2 presents a sample calculation of weighted-risk assets and shows the effect of risk weighting. Except for banks with large "off-balance sheet" asset positions, risk weighting will nearly always lower total assets requiring capital support. However, even if a bank held nothing but cash and U.S. securities, it would still be required to maintain capital support for these assets. The reason is that banks face more than credit risk (for example, liquidity, market, and operational risks), and these other risks require that capital be kept at some minimum level to protect the bank and its depositors.[4]

29

Table 2.1

COMPONENTS OF CAPITAL*

Components	Minimum requirements
CORE CAPITAL (Tier 1)	**Must equal or exceed 4 percent of weighted-risk assets**
Common stockholders' equity	No limit
Qualifying noncumulative perpetual preferred stock	No limit; banks should avoid undue reliance on preferred stock in Tier 1.
Minority interest in equity accounts of consolidated subsidiaries	Bank should avoid using minority interests to introduce elements not otherwise qualifying for Tier 1 capital.
Less: goodwill and all identifiable intangibles[1]	
SUPPLEMENTARY CAPITAL (Tier 2)	**Total of Tier 2 is limited to 100 percent of Tier 1**[2]
Allowance for loan and lease losses	Limited to 1.25 percent of weighted-risk assets[2]
Perpetual preferred stock and related surplus	No limit within Tier 2
Hybrid capital instruments and mandatory convertible debt securities	No limit within Tier 2
Term subordinated debt and intermediate-term preferred stock, including related surplus	Subordinated debt and intermediate-term preferred stock are limited to 50 percent of Tier 1[2], amortized for capital purposes as they approach maturity.
Revaluation reserves (equity and building)	Not included; banks encouraged to disclose; may be evaluated on a case-by-case basis for international comparisons; taken into account in making an overall assessment of capital.
Unrealized holding gains on equity securities	Limited to 45 percent of pre-tax net unrealized gain on available-for-sale equity securities with readily determinable fair values.

Table 2.1

Components	Minimum requirements
DEDUCTIONS (from sum of Tier 1 and Tier 2) Investments in unconsolidated subsidiaries	Generally, one-half of aggregate investments is deducted from Tier 1 capital, the other half from Tier 2[3].
Reciprocal holdings of banking organizations' capital securities Other deductions (such as other subsidiaries or joint ventures) as determined by supervisory authority	On a case-by-case basis as a matter of policy after formal rule making
TOTAL CAPITAL (Tier 1 + Tier 2 - Deductions)	Must equal or exceed 8 percent of weighted-risk assets

*Capital Adequacy Guidelines (Washington, D.C.: Board of Governors of the Federal Reserve System) May, 2002, p. 35. Note: Bank capital structure may also have a Tier 3 capital component. This is a form of debt capital with restrictions on such matters as its original maturity, redemption, and interest and principal payments. It may be used to provide capital support for market risk at a bank with significant trading activities. It is not meant to be used to support a bank's credit risk.

[1]Requirements for the deduction of goodwill, other intangible assets, credit enhancing strips, and some nonfinancial equity investments are set forth in the capital regulations. Note: Some intangibles are grandfathered for state member banks.

[2]Amounts in excess of limitations are permitted but do not qualify as capital.

[3]A proportionally greater amount may be deducted from Tier 1 capital if the risks associated with subsidiary so warrant.

31

Table 2.2

SAMPLE WEIGHTED-RISK ASSET CALCULATION

Bank asset	Asset amount	Risk weight	Weighted-risk asset
Cash	$5,000	.0	$ 0
Balances at domestic banks	5,000	.20	1,000
Loans secured by first lien on 1-to-4 family residential property	5,000	.50	2,500
Loans to private corporations	65,000	1.00	65,000
Total	$80,000		$68,500

The federal banking agencies use several ratio measures to assess the adequacy of a bank's capital. For a bank to be adequately capitalized, it must have total capital-to-weighted-risk assets of at least 8 percent. Additionally, it must have at least a 4 percent Tier I capital-to-weighted-risk assets ratio and a 4 percent Tier I capital-to-average total assets ratio (leverage ratio). The agencies caution, however, that banks should keep their capital above regulatory minimums, especially if they face inordinate risks or contemplate significant asset growth or expansion.

Capital adequacy takes on an added dimension with the establishment of a formal system of prompt corrective action under the Federal Deposit Insurance Corporation Improvement Act of 1991 (FDICIA). This system uses bank capital levels to trigger supervisory actions designed to quickly correct banking problems. Table 2.3 presents the capital adequacy zones used by the federal banking agencies to trigger these actions. The ratios and the definition of "adequate capital" (refer to line two in the table) are the same as those used by the agencies in their capital adequacy guidelines.

Table 2.3

CAPITAL ADEQUACY ZONES—PROMPT CORRECTIVE ACTION

Capital adequacy zones	Total risk-based ratio	Tier 1 risk-based ratio	Leverage ratio
Well capitalized*	10% or more **and****	6% or more **and**	5% or more
Adequately capitalized	8% or more **and**	4% or more **and**	4% or more***
Undercapitalized	Less than 8% **or**	Less than 4% **or**	Less than 4%†
Significantly undercapitalized	Less than 6% **or**	Less than 3% **or**	Less than 3%
Critically undercapitalized	–	–	Less than 2%‡

*In addition to meeting ratio tests, a bank, to be well capitalized, must not be subject to regulatory written agreement, order, capital directive, or prompt corrective action directive.

**The words "and" or "or" in the table mean that a bank must meet all three capital ratio tests to be considered "well" or "adequately" capitalized, or meet any one of the ratio tests to be considered undercapitalized.

***3 percent or more if the bank is rated composite 1 in its most recent report of examination and meets other conditions (for example, is not anticipating or experiencing significant growth and is well diversified, has excellent asset quality, has high liquidity, has good earnings, and has no undue interest-rate risk exposure).

†Less than 3 percent if the bank is rated composite 1 in its most recent report of examination and meets other criteria (for example, is not anticipating or experiencing significant growth and is well diversified, has excellent asset quality, has high liquidity, has good earnings, and has no undue interest-rate risk exposure).

‡For critically undercapitalized banks, this ratio is defined as core capital, plus cumulative perpetual preferred less all but certain intangible items, to total assets.

Under prompt corrective action, banks that are inadequately capitalized face a variety of mandatory and discretionary supervisory actions. For example, "undercapitalized banks" must restrict asset growth, obtain prior approval for business expansion, and have an approved plan to restore capital. "Critically undercapitalized banks" must be placed in receivership or conservatorship within 90 days unless some other action would result in lower long-term costs to the deposit insurance fund. In addition to mandatory actions, the agencies have discretion to require inadequately capitalized banks to, among other things, limit dividend payments, limit deposit rates paid, replace senior executive officers, and elect new directors.

Planning for the Bank's Capital Needs

As mentioned at the outset, you have a major responsibility for ensuring that your bank is adequately capitalized. Fulfilling this responsibility, however, encompasses more than making sure the bank meets regulatory guidelines. It requires considering a wide range of matters that may call on the bank's capital resources. Additionally, it requires developing plans for building capital resources to meet these calls. In order to assess your bank's capital needs, you need to know its current position and the adequacy of that position in protecting the bank, now and in the future. Accordingly, you need to be familiar with the level and trend in your bank's financial condition. Additionally, you must be familiar with the bank's plans and strategies for the future and how these may affect capital adequacy. For example, if your bank has a high level of problem loans and this level is growing over time, capital will need to be bolstered to support greater possible future charge-offs. If your bank plans to make significant acquisitions, to rapidly increase assets, to start new business activities, or to make significant additions or changes to facilities, added capital will be needed to support these efforts. Also, if your bank's strategy is to emphasize lending or to specialize in lending to a few industries, additional capital will be required to compensate for the concentration risk these strategies may pose.

Besides determining capital needs, you and other directors, together with management, must develop plans to raise needed capital. These plans may use a variety of strategies to keep the bank's capital position strong. For example, one strategy may call for strengthening capital by tapping external sources. Another may call for building capital internally through earnings retention or using a combination of external and internal capital sources. Alternatively, plans may call for lessening the need for capital by selling assets or by replacing higher risk assets with lower risk assets.

External sources of capital

Whether or not a bank can raise capital from external sources depends upon a number of factors. Two of the most important of these are the bank's financial condition and size. Financially sound banks or banks that are subsidiaries of strong bank holding companies generally can find purchasers for their equity and debt capital issues. On the other hand, banks or companies that are in poor or deteriorating condition generally may find few takers for their stock issues and debt instruments.

Size can be another important factor in funding capital needs from external sources. For example, larger banks and companies may have better access to capital markets, giving them more options for raising capital. Smaller institutions, on the other hand, may have fewer options, requiring them to rely to a large extent on the "deep pockets" of their owners for capital injections.

Internal sources of capital

Another method for building capital is through earnings retention. Depending upon your bank's circumstances, this may require making some hard choices. For example, bank dividends may have to be reduced or eliminated until capital is restored to sound levels even though this may cause possible financial hardship for owners who rely on dividends as an income source or for the parent bank holding company that relies on dividends to service debt.[5] Or, if your bank's earnings power is low, it may mean reducing asset growth, abandoning planned acquisitions, and putting on hold branch additions and other facilities improvements.

Selling assets and reducing credit risk

An alternative to raising capital is to reduce the need for capital by selling assets or by redistributing asset holdings to those requiring less capital support. In following this strategy, your bank may be able to sell assets to others, thereby reducing the asset base on which capital must be held. Additionally, your bank might redistribute its asset portfolio, moving to lower weighted-risk assets (for example, reducing loans in favor of U.S. government securities), which require less capital.

Some banking analysts view these approaches as a less desirable way to restore a bank's capital position. For example, they argue that asset sales, especially loans, may result in the loss of good customers to those who purchase the loans. In addition, they note asset sales may leave a bank with poorer quality and less liquid assets since purchasers may only be interested in a bank's highest quality, most readily marketable assets. They also note that portfolio shifts may lower earnings as the bank moves away from higher risk, higher yielding assets (for example, loans) to lower risk, lower yielding assets (such as U.S. government securities).

In summary, evaluating and planning for a bank's capital needs is a major responsibility for directors. To carry out this responsibility, directors must monitor their bank's capital position on an ongoing basis and identify factors that may influence the adequacy of this position over time. It also requires that the directorate work with management to develop strategies to meet identified needs.

Monitoring Capital Adequacy

A useful tool for evaluating your bank's capital position, as well as other areas of performance, is financial ratio analysis. A principal benefit of using ratios to analyze performance is that they provide information that dollar values may not. For example, if during the course of a board meeting you were told that your bank's equity capital doubled over an operating period, you may conclude that the bank has strengthened its capital position. However, if over the same period the bank's assets tripled, you would conclude that capital support actually declined. Financial ratios facilitate making these comparisons.

Current period values for financial ratios can be made more meaningful if they are placed in context. For example, comparisons with historical ratio values place your bank's performance in context with its past operation. With this information you can address questions such as "Is the bank's capital position improving?" "Is it deteriorating?" or "If the changes I see continue, will my bank's capital be sufficient for safe and sound operation?"

Comparison with budget and peer information also can be helpful.[6] These comparisons can help answer such questions as "Is the bank's capital position where we planned it to be?" or "Is our capital position on par with similarly situated banks?"

Table 2.4 on the following page presents ratios commonly used to monitor bank capital. The first three are the same ratios you saw earlier in Table 2.3 and are included as tools to assess compliance with capital adequacy guidelines. The last three ratios take into account factors that may temper your bank's capital needs. In this regard, ratios four and five provide insights regarding asset and capital growth at your bank. The last ratio gives an indication of a bank's ability to fund asset growth internally through earnings retention.

In conclusion, bank capital serves many of the same purposes as capital in any other business. However, because bank capital protects depositors and reduces the loss exposure of the federal safety net for banks, bank capital levels are subject to regulatory guidelines. It is an important director responsibility to make sure that cushion remains strong. This requires monitoring the bank's capital position closely, anticipating capital needs, and planning ways to meet those needs.

Table 2.4

RATIO ANALYSIS—CAPITAL

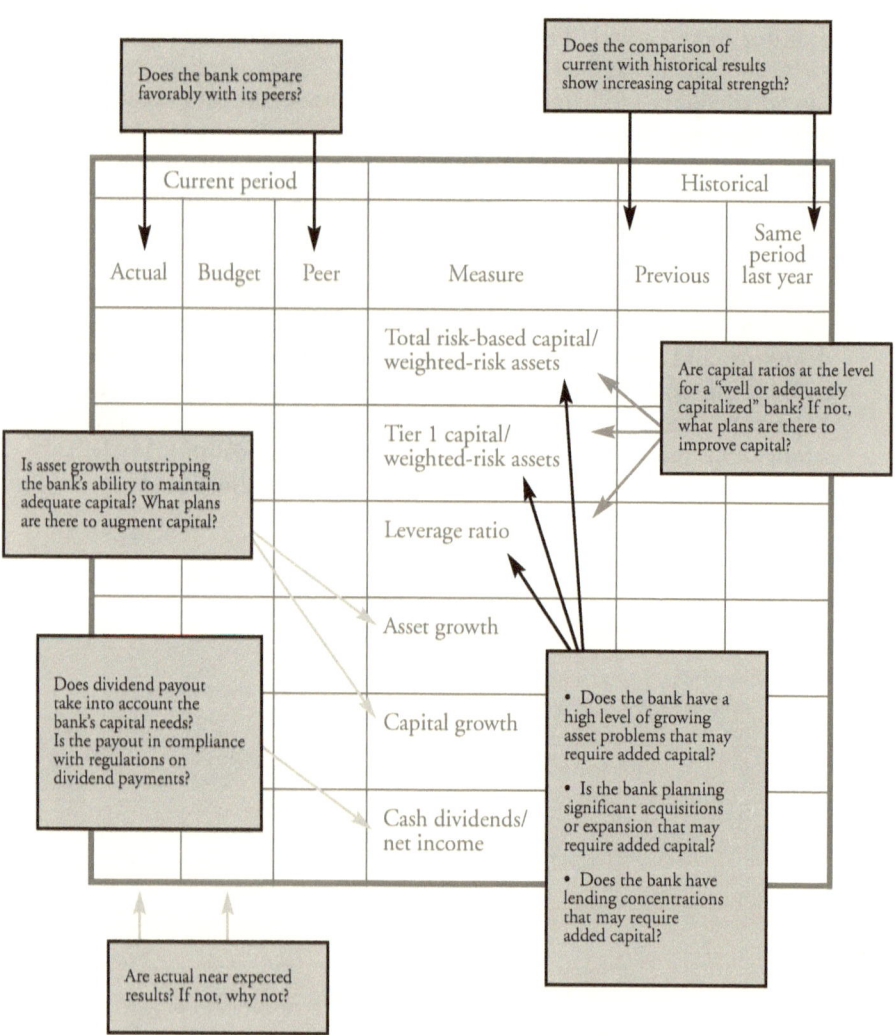

ASSET QUALITY

Asset quality refers to the amount of risk or "probable" loss in a bank's assets and the strength of management processes to control credit risk. Where these losses are judged to be small and management processes are strong, asset quality is considered good. Where losses are large and management processes are weak, asset quality is considered poor.

A bank can suffer asset losses in many ways. For example, it may experience loan losses because of borrower unwillingness or inability to repay. The bank may see a decline in the value of its other real estate holdings because of poor market conditions. It may suffer depreciation in its securities holdings because of market interest rate changes or issuer default. Additionally, it may experience losses from theft or incur losses on deposits held at other financial institutions that fail.

Of these losses, the greatest concern is with those associated with credit quality in the loan portfolio. This is because most bank failures occur because of loan problems.[7] Loans typically constitute a majority of a bank's assets (Chart 2.2), and interest earned on loans is an important source of a bank's revenues. Consequently, even relatively small problems in a bank's loan portfolio can quickly reduce earnings, deplete capital, and cause insolvency.

Chart 2.2

BANK ASSET COMPOSITION ALL U.S. BANKS–2003

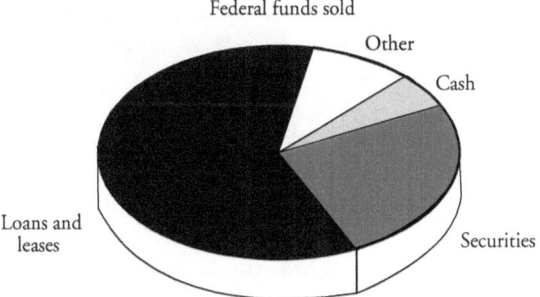

Source: Reports of Condition and Income

39

Over time, various lending practices have been associated with greater credit risk for banks. For example, studies show that lax lending policies, excessive loans to insiders, and concentrations of credit can lead to loan problems and bank failure. Because of this, laws and regulations address many of these known lending "trouble spots," and examiners during the course of their review look for regulatory compliance. Additionally, they scrutinize loan policies, loan review, loan documentation and administration, and loan monitoring during bank examinations, looking for weaknesses in the lending function.

Despite restrictions, banks have considerable latitude in their lending. As a director, it is one of your duties to ensure that lending is done responsibly and with concern for bank soundness, shareholder returns, and community credit needs. In carrying out your duties, you may occasionally participate directly in making significant lending decisions. Other times you may play a more indirect, but just as important, role setting lending policies for the bank and reviewing, approving, and monitoring the loan decisions of others.

This section discusses bank asset quality, focusing on the quality of the loan portfolio. It discusses possible causes of loan problems and methods typically used by banks to manage loan quality. It also discusses some tools you may find useful for monitoring asset quality.

Sources of Asset Quality Problems

Banks face a variety of risks in managing their loans. Among these are:

Credit risk—the risk that borrowers are unable or unwilling to repay the principal and interest associated with their debt obligations to the bank.

Interest rate risk—the risk that interest rate movements may change bank asset and liability values or reduce the spread between asset returns and asset funding costs.

Liquidity risk—the risk that the bank may not have sufficient funds to meet its cash needs.

Of these, credit risk is generally the main concern when banks evaluate lending opportunities.[8] Judging this risk and pricing for it is the principal business of banks. How well an individual bank does this job largely determines its profitability and viability.

The effectiveness of a bank in controlling its credit risk exposure depends upon a number of factors. Important among these are the bank's lending policies and its credit underwriting standards. Experience shows that where policies are not specified and underwriting standards are not enforced, loan problems generally ensue and loan losses occur.

The Loan Policy

Decisions regarding extensions of credit, loan review, allowance for loan and lease losses, and charge-offs are all important matters that should be addressed by written policies. Implementing and adhering to these policies provide objective criteria for evaluating individual credit decisions and help promote consistency and stability in the lending function. In doing so, lending policies help a bank avoid pitfalls that may lead to loan problems.

Because a bank's lending function has operational ramifications for the entire bank, it is important that lending policies take into consideration the broader needs of the bank. Examples of matters that should be factored in are the bank's orientation (for example, business versus consumer lending), trade area, size, facilities, personnel, and financial resources. The customer base within the bank's trade area, the number of competitors it faces, and the state of the local and national economy should also be considered. It is fairly easy to see why close attention to these matters is important in guiding a bank's lending decisions. For example, if a bank's strategy calls for it to be a consumer bank, then its lending policies should emphasize installment lending with less attention given to commercial or real estate lending. Or, if the bank's strategy is to actively pursue a specialized type of lending activity, then it should make sure it has the facilities and the qualified staff necessary to support this type of lending.

Today, almost all banks operate with written loan policies. The details covered in these policies tend to vary among banks, depending upon individual needs and circumstances. Despite this, bank loan policies tend to have common elements. For example, policies almost always set out objectives to be accomplished. Basic objectives often found are:

- Granting loans on a sound and collectible basis;

- Investing the bank's funds profitably for the benefit of shareholders and the protection of depositors; and

- Serving the legitimate credit needs of the bank's community.

Additionally, most policies spell out the scope of the bank's lending activities (for example, where it will make loans, maximum size and types of loans it will make, and the terms on which it will make those loans), and how loans will be made, serviced, and collected. Additionally, they address "who will grant credit, in what amount, and what organizational structure will be used to ensure compliance with the bank's guidelines and procedures."[9] Table 2.5 summarizes many of the factors covered by loan policies.

The Allowance for Loan and Lease Losses (ALLL)

Besides the loan policy, an important consideration in managing bank asset quality is the ALLL. The ALLL is a bank's best estimate of the amount it will not be able to collect on its loans and leases based on current information and events. To fund the ALLL, the bank takes periodic charges against earnings, the provision for loan and lease losses. When loan losses occur, the bank charges them to the ALLL. Thus, the ALLL provides a protective cushion for bank capital and an additional layer of depositor protection. If a bank's reserving methodology is inaccurate, loans on its books are carried at inflated values and earnings and capital are overstated.

Table 2.5

MATTERS OFTEN CONSIDERED IN A LOAN POLICY

- The proportion of loans by type (agriculture, commercial, consumer, real estate) in the loan portfolio and the maximum amount the bank will commit to a single borrower, groups of borrowers, or industries.
- The geographic area in which the bank will ordinarily lend.
- Minimum documentation, acceptable financial ratios, and other factors considered by the bank in extending credit.
- Requirements and limitation on loans to "insiders" and their related interests.
- Acceptable types of loans and loan collateral.
- Collateral appraisal standards and who can perform appraisals.
- Pricing, structure, and other loan terms, including maximum loan term.
- Limits on renewals and extensions, including specific criteria for additional lending to problem borrowers.
- Periodic review, inspection, and administration of loans after disbursement.
- Criteria for collecting delinquent loans and charging off loans.
- Procedures for exceptions to the loan policy.
- Reports to the board of directors.
- Loan policy review by the board of directors.

To provide for a consistently determined, adequate ALLL, bank boards often use an ALLL policy. Generally, this policy establishes:

- Lines of responsibility for determining an adequate reserve for the bank.

- The bank's loan loss methodology.

- The bank's loan review system, including its loan grading system, and responsibilities for its implementation.

- Criteria and procedures for charging-off and collecting on charged-off loans.

- Reports and communication channels among those involved in the ALLL determination process.

- Periodic independent review of the ALLL determination process for compliance with policy, adequacy with respect to the bank's charge-off history, changes in the size and complexity of its lending, and consistency with accounting and supervisory guidance.

- The periodic review of the ALLL policy by the board of directors.

Because of the importance of ALLL, the federal banking agencies have issued policy statements providing guidance on ALLL methodologies and documentation. The current framework dates back to 1993 and requires that the ALLL be determined in accordance with generally accepted accounting principles (GAAP) and supervisory guidance. In the past, however, there has been some controversy over what constitutes an appropriate ALLL, and as a result, the federal banking agencies published additional guidance further clarifying their expectations regarding ALLL methodologies and documentation. This guidance was issued in July 2001.[10]

Under the guidance, the ALLL is made up mainly of two components. The first component includes the estimated loss in impaired credits. The estimated losses in these credits constitute the FAS 114 portion of the ALLL (FAS 114 refers to Financial Accounting Board Statement Number 114, *Accounting by Creditors for Impairment of a Loan,* which provides accounting guidance for determining the amount for this part of the reserve). The second component, the FAS 5 (*Accounting for Contingencies*) component, includes the estimated loss in the remainder of the bank's portfolio.

As a director, you are responsible for ensuring that the ALLL is kept at an adequate level and that this level is determined consistently and in compliance with accounting and supervisory guidance. Additionally, you have responsibility for periodic review of the bank's ALLL methodology and any supporting documentation to determine if adjustments and changes are needed, and, at least annually, provide for the independent validation of the bank's ALLL methodology and ALLL adequacy.

Although it is unlikely you will actually develop the data for the components that make up your bank's ALLL balance, basic information about the general framework on which its ALLL methodology is based may help you in establishing policies that provide staff guidance for determining an adequate reserve, assist in your quarterly review of the reserve's adequacy, and aid in determining if changes should be made in the bank's reserve methodology and its supporting documentation. Table 2.6 summarizes the framework outlined by the banking agencies in their policy guidance for the ALLL, setting out steps used to calculate the FAS 114 and FAS 5 portions of the ALLL.

It is important to remember that determining an adequate ALLL for your bank requires a considerable amount of judgment. In the end, it represents management's best estimate, given facts and circumstances when the estimate was made, of potential loss in the bank's loan portfolio. To achieve consistency in this estimate requires policy guidance, supporting written documentation, and periodic review to validate and assess the need for changes in determining the bank's ALLL balance.

Monitoring Bank Asset Quality

Given the significance of credit risk to a bank's financial condition, it is important that you monitor the level and trend in loan quality and assess the adequacy of the ALLL at your bank to judge the effectiveness of policies in managing asset quality. To do this, you can draw upon a number of information sources. These sources include financial statements prepared by the bank; reports developed by the bank's lending, loan review, and internal audit functions; and reports developed by independent parties, external to the bank. The bank's financial statements can be used to construct broad asset quality measures for comparing its current loan quality with planned and historic figures and with quality at other banks. Table 2.7 provides frequently used ratios to judge asset quality and reserve adequacy.

Table 2.6

FRAMEWORK FOR DETERMINING AN ADEQUATE ALLL

A bank's ALLL balance consists primarily of a FAS 114 component and a FAS 5 component. In their July 2001 policy guidance, the banking agencies discussed matters to consider in constructing each component and provided suggestions and examples of documentation to support a bank's ALLL methodology. The following briefly summarizes the framework provided by the banking agencies to determine the FAS 114 and FAS 5 components of the reserve.

There are three steps to estimating the FAS 114 portion of a bank's reserve. The first step requires identifying loans that are to be evaluated separately for estimated loss. For instance, a bank may evaluate all loans above a certain size or loans above a certain percentage of its capital for impairment under FAS 114, hereafter referred to as FAS 114 loans. Or, it may designate loans identified through its loan review as requiring special attention by management to be evaluated separately for impairment. Regardless of the way the bank identifies FAS 114 loans in the portfolio, the method and process it uses to identify these loans should be documented in writing.

The second step requires determining if the previously identified FAS 114 loans are impaired and, if so, the amount of impairment. Impaired loans are those where it is probable (is likely to occur), given current information and events, that the bank will not receive contractual principal and interest when due. Once the bank's analysis establishes which of its FAS 114 loans are impaired, the amount of impairment is determined. This is done by assigning all impaired FAS 114 loans to one of three categories (collateral dependent, saleable loans, cash flow loans) and comparing their fair value with that on the bank's books. Collateral dependent loans are those where payment may come solely from collateral pledged to the bank in the event of borrower default. A vast majority of loans at most banks are made with some form of collateral support so that the impairment in them will make up a significant part of the estimated reserve balance.

The fair value for collateral dependent loans is the appraised value of the collateral adjusted for such things as holding costs before the

Table 2.6 (continued)

collateral is sold, maintenance cost during the period the bank expects to hold the collateral, selling costs, and any other economic or financial factors that may influence the realizable value from the sale.

Saleable loans are those that have an observable market price. The fair value of these loans is what an independent third party, in an arms length transaction, would be willing to pay for them.

Cash flow loans make up the rest of the portfolio. The fair value of these loans is the sum of the present values of their discounted expected cash flows over their projected lives, taking into account the effective discount rate and factors that may affect the amount and timing in cash flows.

As was the case in the first step, the analysis done to determine impairment and rationale for the measurement method used to estimate the amount of impairment in each FAS 114 loan category should be documented in writing to support calculations made.

The third step requires calculating the FAS 114 amount for the reserve. This is done by summing, within each category, the difference between the book value and the fair value of all loans whose fair value is less than book value. The total of the category sums represents the FAS 114 component of the ALLL.

The FAS 5 component of the ALLL consists of loans that are evaluated on a group basis. There are three basic steps for developing this amount of the reserve as well. The first step requires segmenting the non-FAS 114 portion of the portfolio into homogenous groups with similar risk characteristics (for example, by agriculture, business, consumer, and real estate loans). One segment may also include FAS 114 loans that were not found to be impaired in the bank's FAS 114 analysis but may still include some potential loss. For these loan groups, the idea is that the probability of loss is not associated with an individual credit. Instead, within the group of loans, the bank may experience some amount of loss. The basis or the rationale for the segments the bank uses should be documented.

Continued on following page

Table 2.6 (continued)

The second step in determining the FAS 5 component is to apply a loss factor to each loan segment. These loss factors can be based on a bank's own historical experience adjusted for such things as: level and trend of delinquencies and impaired loans, levels and trends in charge-offs and recoveries; changes in lending philosophy and underwriting standards; changes in experience, ability, and depth of lending management or other relevant staff; national and local economic trends and conditions; and the effects of credit concentrations. If a bank does not have loss experience of its own, it may use that of other banks that have portfolio segments with similar risk attributes. Regardless of the source of loss rates, the bank needs to provide the supporting rationale for the rates it uses. It should provide information about the time frames over which the rates are calculated, support adjustments it makes to those rates, and document that the loss rates it uses are in accordance with GAAP.

The third step requires calculating the FAS 5 component of the reserve. This is done by simply adding the estimated loss for each segment. Once calculated, the FAS 5 component is added to the FAS 114 component to provide an estimated ALLL balance.

Table 2.7

RATIO ANALYSIS—ASSET QUALITY

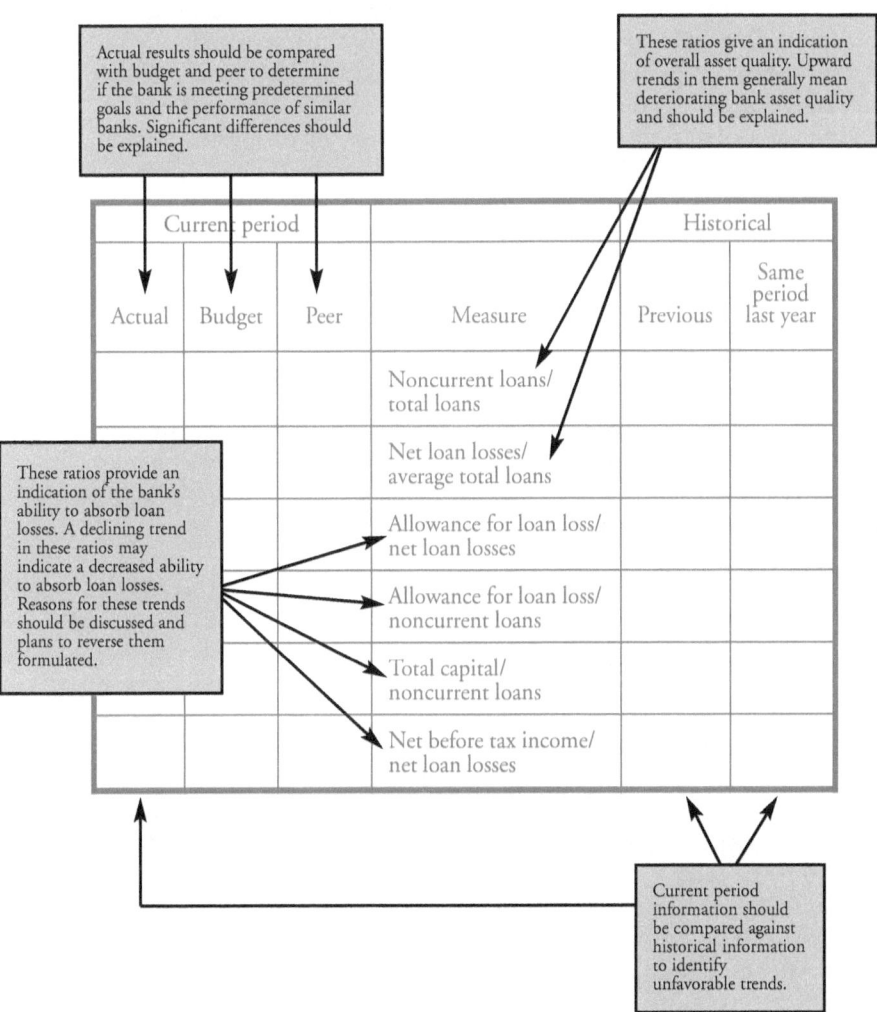

Actual results should be compared with budget and peer to determine if the bank is meeting predetermined goals and the performance of similar banks. Significant differences should be explained.

These ratios give an indication of overall asset quality. Upward trends in them generally mean deteriorating bank asset quality and should be explained.

These ratios provide an indication of the bank's ability to absorb loan losses. A declining trend in these ratios may indicate a decreased ability to absorb loan losses. Reasons for these trends should be discussed and plans to reverse them formulated.

Current period information should be compared against historical information to identify unfavorable trends.

| Current period | | | | Historical | |
Actual	Budget	Peer	Measure	Previous	Same period last year
			Noncurrent loans/ total loans		
			Net loan losses/ average total loans		
			Allowance for loan loss/ net loan losses		
			Allowance for loan loss/ noncurrent loans		
			Total capital/ noncurrent loans		
			Net before tax income/ net loan losses		

Besides financial statements, there are other information sources that you can draw upon to judge the management of your bank's credit risk. For example, many banks internally grade their loans. These grades are often used to create a "problem loan" or "watch list" of credits that may pose above-normal credit risk that deserve special attention by management. You should review this list periodically and ask yourself: "Is the list growing or shrinking with time?"; "If it is growing, what is the reason behind the growth?"; "Is there a written plan to collect fully or minimize the bank's loss on each listed credit?"; "Is progress being shown in collecting credits listed?"; and "Does the list show signs of poor problem loan identification?" (for example, are loans listed in one period and charged off the next?).

Additionally, you can use watch list information to construct two benchmark ratios used by examiners as part of their assessment of your bank's asset quality. The gross classification ratio is the sum of all loans from the watch list rated substandard or doubtful (if your bank uses numerical ratings, ask management to translate these ratings into the substandard and doubtful classifications used by examiners) divided by the sum of the bank's Tier 1 capital and ALLL. The federal and most state banking agencies use this ratio.

The weighted classification ratio used by the Federal Reserve is another ratio you can use to do a self-assessment of your bank's asset quality. In computing this ratio, problem loans are weighted according to their severity—loss loans are multiplied by 1.0, doubtful loans are multiplied by .5, and substandard loans by .2. Their sum is divided by the bank's Tier 1 capital plus ALLL. For example, if a bank's doubtful loans on its watch list were $800, its substandard loans were $200, and its Tier 1 capital plus ALLL were $4,400, its weighted classification ratio would be 10 percent (.5x$800+.2x$200=$440; $440 /$4,400= .10 or 10 percent). Values nearing 40 percent for the gross classification ratio and 15 percent for the weighted classification ratio may be indicators of less than satisfactory asset quality. However, you shouldn't wait until ratio values reach these levels before asking management about its plans for addressing loan quality at your bank. The fact that the ratios are rising and moving toward these values should be enough to trigger your concern and questions to management. One last point, notice in the sample calculation that there was no mention of loss loans. The reason for this is that when a bank recognizes a loan as loss, the bank should charge it off. Consequently, the weighted ratio calculated by the bank should have no loss loans included in it. If it does, a good question to ask management is why the loans haven't been charged off.

Besides the watch list, there are reports on new loans, delinquent credits, nonaccrual loans, restructured loans, charge-offs, overdrafts, and transactions with insiders and their related interests that may give you insights regarding potential loan problems and management's speed and effectiveness in addressing those problems. In looking at these reports, you may want management to explain sudden and large movements in items listed. Also, you may want to compare reports, looking for borrowers that appear on multiple reports, or you may want to track reports over time to see if the same borrowers reappear. Once again, you may want management to explain circumstances pertaining to these borrowers.

Internal and external audit reports are another useful information source for keeping abreast of asset quality at your bank. The federal banking agencies encourage all institutions to establish some form of internal audit function to inform directors and senior management of the adequacy, effectiveness, and efficiency of accounting, operating, and administrative controls and to provide an assessment of the quality of ongoing operations. This function may identify weaknesses in and noncompliance with lending policies and procedures, and make recommendations on matters to be corrected. In addition, the directorate itself is sometimes required by the bank's bylaws or by banking law to perform a "directors' examination" to keep itself informed about the bank. This examination may include an evaluation of the bank's financial condition and the adequacy of its reserves. Similarly, audits and asset/operational reviews performed by accounting firms, consulting firms, and others may help identify policy compliance weaknesses, provide data on loan quality, furnish an assessment of the bank's loan review system, determine the adequacy of its loan administration, and give an indication of loan documentation inadequacies.

Finally, bank examination reports are a valuable source of information on the bank's lending function. Among other things, examiners review asset quality, ALLL adequacy, loan review adequacy, loan policy adherence, and credit administration effectiveness. They also provide an overall assessment of a bank's ability to identify, administer, and collect problem credits. In using your bank's examination reports to gauge its asset quality, you may want to compare the level and severity of loan classifications with internally generated loan grades as a form of "reality check." Additionally, you may want to ask management to address any examiner comments calling for increased reserves and for improving loan policies and credit administration. If you see repeat criticisms on these and other matters pertaining to the lending function in the bank's examination reports, you should ask management for specific plans to address the criticisms and monitor implementation of plans to correct them.

In summary, bank directors are responsible for asset quality and for ensuring their banks maintain an adequate reserve to absorb loan losses. To do this, you and other board members should establish policies to guide the bank's lending activities. Additionally, you should put in place policies and processes to determine probable loss in the loan portfolio and to maintain an adequate reserve to cover these losses. Finally, you should monitor asset quality and the adequacy of the reserve to ensure that policies in place are effective in preserving bank asset quality and cushioning the bank against foreseeable losses.

MANAGEMENT

Management refers to a host of factors necessary to operate a bank in a safe and sound manner. It includes the quality and character of individuals who guide and supervise the bank, encompassing their: knowledge, experience, and technical expertise; leadership, organizational, and administrative skills; planning skills and adaptability; and honesty and integrity. It also encompasses the policies, procedures, and controls these individuals have put in place to protect the bank from excessive risk and the systems they have installed to provide feedback on the bank's financial and operational status.

This section discusses the director's role as part of the bank's management team. It sets out director responsibilities as part of this team and suggests matters to consider in judging bank management performance.

Director's Role

Your bank is a corporation organized and chartered under state or national law. Like other corporations, it is managed under the oversight of a board of directors that is elected by its shareholders. The board normally delegates the authority and responsibility for running the bank on a daily basis to its officers. Despite this, you, as a director, ultimately remain accountable to the bank's shareholders and other stakeholders—employees, depositors, and community—for its safe, sound, and efficient operation.[11]

In seeing to these responsibilities, you, as a board member, owe your bank the "duty of care," "duty of obedience," and "duty of loyalty." Duty of care means that you will devote time, exercise ordinary diligence, and use reasonable judgment to ensure your bank is run prudently and with due regard for the bank's stakeholders.[12] Duty of obedience means you will obey applicable laws in your personal dealings with the bank and ensure that your bank complies with laws and regulations. Duty of loyalty means you will not engage in activities or make use of information obtained as a director that benefits you at the expense of your bank.

Beyond these basic obligations, there is no single definitive list that sets out the basic responsibilities for the board of directors and its members. However, several key responsibilities seem to appear on more lists than others and they are included here. Among these are the responsibilities to:

Provide the bank with competent management

Directors are charged with providing the bank with capable management. If management is poor, all areas of the bank's operations suffer. Moreover, if management is poor, you and other board members will have to spend considerable time and effort to correct problems in order to restore the bank to a satisfactory condition.

As noted earlier, providing the bank with competent management does not mean that individual board members take responsibility for running the bank's daily operation. That is not a director's job. Instead, board members are charged with the responsibility of providing a bank with a competent CEO to manage its daily operations, advising that management, and making sure succession plans are in place to provide for the bank's future management. Along with this, the board has the important duty of periodically evaluating management's performance in running the bank.

Plan for the bank

It is important that the board set long-term direction and goals for a bank to make sure there is an orderly transition from where the bank is today to where it will be tomorrow. Providing long-term direction helps the bank identify financial and personnel resources and technological and organizational capabilities needed to meet its goals. It also provides management a guide that can be used to compare shorter-term decisions for their consistency with the bank's longer-term goals and helps management budget resources to move the bank progressively toward long-term objectives. Because of this, decisions that represent major changes in direction or philosophy from the bank's established plan should be given careful consideration since they often carry resource implications for the bank.

In addition to long-term planning, the board has responsibility for making sure the bank has adequate plans and backup procedures in place to address operational contingencies such as destruction of its building or failure of its automated systems.

Set out clear policies and monitor the bank's operations for compliance

Another key responsibility of directors is to establish written operating policies covering such facets of the bank's operations as lending, allowance for loan and lease losses, investments, funding, liquidity, and asset/liability mix. These policies establish risk limits and an operating framework for guiding the bank's operation. Invariably, in the past when a bank experienced difficulty, it was because it had no or few written operating policies, its policies were not appropriate given the size and complexity of the bank's operations, or its policies were frequently overridden or ignored.

Besides establishing policies, it is important that the board, in conjunction with senior management, establish the necessary internal controls to provide feedback on compliance and adequacy of policies put in place. Where deficiencies are noted, the board should ask for management's plans to address them and track management's progress in completing its plan.

Know where the bank stands

To be effective, it is important you remain knowledgeable about the bank's financial condition and the adequacy of its internal controls. Studies of failed banks show that many were governed by inattentive, uninformed, or passive directorates. As a result, many trouble signs went unrecognized until it was too late and the banks failed.

Keeping up with the bank requires the board to specify reports it needs for tracking the bank's progress and to study these reports. Additionally, it is important that the board independently verify the information it receives through the use of internal and external audits and examination reports. This is not to imply that management is dishonest or lacks integrity. It is simply a good business practice and a source of protection for the board.

Attend meetings and participate

To remain knowledgeable about the bank's affairs, it is crucial that you attend regular and special board and committee meetings. When attending, you should participate in the deliberations and ask questions if you don't understand what is being presented. For example, if the bank is going to engage in a new lending activity, make "high-risk" investments, or enter into some new nonbanking activity, you might ask at the meeting:

> "Do we really understand the activity and the risks it presents?"

> "What analyses have been done to quantify these risks?"

> "Do we have the personnel and control systems necessary to protect or lessen the bank's exposure to these risks?"

> "Does it make sense for our bank given its size, location, and expertise?"

> "Is the activity or investment consistent with our bank's long-term objectives?"

It is important that you don't blindly accept someone's assurances that "they know what they are doing" or "it's okay." As a director, you need to be an independent thinker and a good questioner. Where your knowledge is limited on matters being addressed, ask for explanations to improve your understanding. If you receive an answer to a question you don't understand, question the answer until you do. After all, you cannot exercise effective oversight of the bank if you don't understand matters being discussed.

It is equally important that the essence or a summary of the board's deliberations, and those of its committees, be recorded in meeting minutes and that you review the minutes from meetings you attend for their accuracy and completeness before you approve them. Minutes are an official record of a bank and play an important role in the supervisory assessment of your bank. During the course of an examination, examiners review all board minutes since the last examination. In broad terms, they use this review to determine if the board of directors is meeting its oversight responsibilities. Among other things, examiners note attendance at board meetings. They look to see if the board has approved business strategies for the bank, approved and reviewed policies that articulate risk tolerances, and set exposure limits for its important activities. They look to see if the board periodically reviewed the bank's performance in order to monitor its risk exposures and effectiveness of its risk management. Additionally, examiners note discussion and resolution of issues on introducing new products, serving new customers, or entering into new geographic areas. They watch for the creation of new committees and the responsibilities given to these committees. In addition, they also look for major board actions that are not part of the normal monthly meeting and board actions that may be in contravention of the bank's bylaws or banking laws and regulations.

In summary, board minutes, as well as all committee minutes, are important. Review them before approving them. This review may pay you dividends later if the bank encounters problems and the board's diligence is questioned. Otherwise, the record won't be there when you need it most. As one examiner put it, "If it's not in the minutes, it didn't happen."

Make sure the bank knows about and helps serve the credit needs of the community

Banks have been and will continue to be vital sources of credit and the engines of economic growth for their communities. As a result, you have responsibility for making sure your bank is an "unbiased" source of credit to the *entire* community. In this regard, you and other board members need to be aware of the economic environment in which your bank operates and be knowledgeable on any special credit needs of the communities it serves.

Although all of a director's duties and responsibilities are important, probably none is more important than providing the bank with competent and capable management. Providing competent management, as previously noted, goes beyond simply hiring qualified officers for the bank. It also requires evaluating the official staff to ensure that the daily supervision and administration of the bank is being done satisfactorily.

Evaluating Bank Management

> *[It is an] inescapable responsibility of directors to see that management is doing its job. The wise choice of capable management and the removal of management that fails the responsibility are true central and culminating responsibilities of the board.*[13]

Evaluating the management of your bank necessitates consideration of many factors and requires that you draw on a number of different sources. Among these sources are the bank's financial statements, internal/external reviews conducted or commissioned by the board, and supervisory examination reports.

Some pundits quip that "nothing speaks more loudly than financial success." Certainly, an important part of your review requires looking at the bank's financial statements. In this review, declines in financial performance and unfavorable comparison with peer banks may be indicators of management inadequacies.[14]

However, financial performance cannot be taken as the sole measure of management performance. Bad management practices can be masked by such things as a strong economy or a strong competitive position. Once conditions reverse or competition strengthens, poor practices are revealed. Thus, another part of your review requires looking beneath the numbers to the organizational and operational matters that produced the bank's operating results. This means trying to understand why the bank performs as it does and determining if that performance is sustainable. It also requires looking to see if the bank has taken on undue risk and determining if management is aware of the risks being taken.

You can glean information on these and other matters relating to the management of your bank from a number of sources. One source is the "director's packet" provided by management at board meetings. Besides financial information, these packets often include lending and securities activity reports, audit and compliance reports, and other reports necessary to monitor bank operations.

Another source is information gathered from the board's own oversight of bank operations. At many banks, directors review loans and other major decisions made by bank officers. At smaller banks, one or more board members may be responsible for conducting these reviews and making periodic reports to the full board. At larger banks, board committees may carry out this review role.

Of the review tools available to the board, the audit is probably the most valuable. The Office of the Comptroller of the Currency and many states require directors to commission an examination of their banks. Additionally, federal and state banking authorities encourage banks to establish an independent audit function that reports directly to the board of directors. Moreover, federal banking law, FDICIA, requires certain insured institutions to establish an independent audit committee made up of outside directors who are independent of management. For larger institutions, the audit committee must include members who have banking or related financial institution expertise. In certain instances, FDICIA requires that insured depository institutions have their financial statements audited by independent public accounting firms in accordance with generally accepted accounting principles.

Bank examination reports are another important information source for judging management. Examination reports discuss adequacy of policies, procedures, and controls, and specifically address the matter of management adequacy, pointing out areas that need improvement (See Box 2.2).

Together, board reviews and examination reports will help you piece together an accurate qualitative picture of management at your bank. As you look over these materials, you may want to consider some of the ideas presented in Table 2.8. It is important to note the checklist items included in the table are only suggestive of things you may want to consider in your review of management. There may be other matters and standards of performance that the board at your bank has adopted for evaluating management.

Box 2.2

OPERATIONS RISK MANAGEMENT: AN INCREASINGLY IMPORTANT MANAGEMENT FACTOR

An important element in examiners' evaluations of bank management is the quality of risk management practices and internal controls.

> *"... it is essential that examiners give significant weight to the quality of risk management practices and internal controls when evaluating management and the overall financial condition of banking organizations ... examiners are ... to assign a formal supervisory rating to the adequacy of an institution's risk processes, including internal controls ... [this rating] should be given considerable weight when evaluating management under the bank (CAMELS) ... [rating system]."**

One area that is receiving increased examiner scrutiny is operations risk management. Operational risk is the risk of loss resulting from inadequate or failed internal processes, people and systems, or from external events. Banks have always managed this risk and banking supervisors have assessed the quality of operations risk practices.

In the past, the primary focus of operations risk reviews was on a bank's internal controls. However, in response to growth in organizational size and complexity; well-publicized losses due to poor internal controls, increased incidence of bank fraud, and proposed support for operational risk in capital adequacy guidelines, banks are taking a more comprehensive approach to managing operations risk. They are treating operating risk management similarly to the way they treat credit, liquidity, and market risk management. Coincidentally, bank supervisors are devoting more examination resources to assessing the adequacy of operations risk management process.

As is the case with management of other risks, operations risk management rests with the board of directors and senior management. The board of directors approves the framework for managing this risk.

Box 2.2 (continued)

Senior management implements the approved framework. Consequently, it is important that you are knowledgeable about sources of the bank's operations risk, the systems and processes in place to control this risk, and feedback mechanisms established to monitor and communicate risk control effectiveness.

Sources of operations risk

A bank faces operations risk from the moment it opens its doors on its first business day to the time it closes those doors on its last business day. Operations risk stems from the very act of being in business and emanates from internal and external events that can harm the bank. Examples of these events include such things as:

- Internal fraud (for example, intentional misreporting of transactions, employee theft).

- External fraud (for example, robbery, forgery, check kiting, and damage from computer hacking).

- Employment practices and workplace safety (for example, compensation claims, violation of employee health and safety rules, organized labor activities, discrimination claims, and general liability–customer slipping and falling on bank property).

- Clients, products, and business practices (for example, misuse of confidential customer information, improper trading activities on the bank's account, money laundering, and sale of unauthorized products).

- Damage or theft to physical assets (for example, loss or damage to physical assets from natural disaster or other events such as terrorism, vandalism, earthquakes, fires and floods).

Continued on following page

Box 2.2 *(continued)*

- Business disruption and system failures (for example, hardware and software failures, telecommunication problems, and utility outages).

- Execution, delivery, and process management (for example, data entry errors, collateral management failures, incomplete legal documentation, unapproved access given to client accounts, non-client counterparty nonperformance, and vendor disputes).**

Identifying these and other sources of risk is a key to effective operations risk management. At many banks, the risk assessment process often starts with individual business units/lines. Managers ask themselves what can go wrong, what is the likelihood or probability it will go wrong, and what is the consequence to the bank if it goes wrong? These assessments flow up through the bank's management ranks where they are aggregated across the organization, resulting in an overall picture of the bank's operating risk exposure.

Operations risk control

Once risk exposures are identified, a decision must be made on the best way to control/reduce them. In this regard, the bank has several options, depending upon its size, expertise, and nature of exposures. For instance, the bank can design and implement controls that reduce the exposures. It can review existing controls to see if they reduce the exposures. It can buy insurance. It can hold additional capital.

Monitoring operations risk

After controls are implemented, it's important to monitor their effectiveness. This requires that the bank's management information system be capable of tracking financial and operating performance data

Box 2.2 *(continued)*

that the board and management feel are key measures to determining the effectiveness of operations risk control.

As you look over and judge the operations risk management process at your bank, here are a few questions you may want to ask yourself or to ask management if you find that you don't know the answers to them. What is our process for identifying the bank's risk exposures? Who has responsibility for performing risk assessments and identifying the bank's exposures? What was the source of loss information—the bank's own experience or from an external loss database? If not from the bank's own experience, is the loss data appropriate for the bank? Who reviews risk assessments and has responsibility for developing the bank's overall risk exposure? Has the assessment process missed any significant risk exposures? Does the bank's loss exposure seem reasonable? What is the bank's risk management strategy for controlling or mitigating the risks it faces? Do these strategies take into account their implications for other risks the bank faces, including credit, liquidity, market, legal, and reputational risks? What measures does the bank use to gauge the effectiveness of strategies followed? Has the internal audit function assessed the bank's operations risk management process for its adequacy in controlling the inherent risk in the bank's activities?

Obtaining answers to these and other questions will help you develop a comfort level with the bank's risk management or reveal possible inadequacies in the bank's processes for identifying, assessing, monitoring, and controlling operations risk.

*SR 95-51(Sup), "Rating the Adequacy of Risk Management Processes and Internal Controls at State Member Banks and Bank Holding Companies," November 14, 1995.

**Basel Committee on Banking Supervision, Bank for International Settlements, *Sound Practices for the Management and Supervision of Operations Risk*, February 2003, p. 2.

Table 2.8

SOME MATTERS TO CONSIDER IN EVALUATING MANAGEMENT

Matter to consider	Yes	No
Is the bank operated in a safe and sound matter?		
Is the bank operated in compliance with laws and regulations?		
Does the bank compare favorably with other banks in major performance areas such capitalization, asset quality, earnings, liquidity, and sensitivity to market risk?		
Does management respond quickly to address shortcomings identified in audits and supervisory examinations?		
Does management keep the board informed and does management provide sufficient and timely information on the bank to enable the board to judge the bank's operational and financial status?		
Are decisions made by management consistent with goals, plans, and policies set out for the bank?		
Does management have the knowledge and expertise to effectively supervise the affairs of the bank and does management instill confidence and demonstrate an ability to lead the bank?		
Is management informed about the affairs of the bank and knowledgeable about events in the community that may affect the bank?		
Has management put in place a corporate structure that establishes lines of authority and accountability; that provide for delegation of authority and monitoring of delegated responsibilities; and that permit open communication and free flow of information within the bank?		
Has management seen to the staffing needs of the bank: established job descriptions, hired qualified staff, offered competitive compensation, provided training, and planned for management succession?		
Has management established information systems to provide timely information on the status of the bank in order to quickly identify evolving problems?		
Has management put in place sufficient procedures to direct the bank's operation and instituted sufficient internal controls to protect the bank's resources?		
Does management plan for the bank and develop reasonable strategies for carrying out these plans?		
Does management, in conjunction with the board, develop budgets for the bank and keep the board informed of the bank's progress in meeting budget goals?		

In summary, the board of directors has many obligations and responsibilities with respect to its bank oversight. The most important of these is to provide the bank with competent management, to evaluate management's performance, and to remove management that fails in its performance.

EARNINGS

Earnings quality refers to the composition, level, trend, and stability of bank profits. For bank directors and managers, earnings quality represents a "financial report card" on how well the bank is doing. When earnings quality is good, the bank has sufficient profits to support operations, provide for asset growth, and build capital. Profits grow over time and show little variability. Moreover, depositors are given an extra margin of protection and shareholders receive a competitive return on their investment. On the other hand, when earnings quality is poor, the bank may not be able to adequately serve the credit needs of the community, provide for losses, or build capital. Moreover, depositors may be at greater risk and shareholder returns may be inadequate.

For you, as a bank director, information on your bank's earnings performance and the factors contributing to that performance are invaluable in ascertaining the effectiveness of its risk management. This information helps pinpoint strengths and weaknesses and is essential to your success in governing the bank and meeting your responsibilities to its stakeholders.

This section looks at the composition of bank earnings and discusses matters that influence earnings performance. It also presents some tools for monitoring and evaluating bank earnings quality.

Composition of Bank Earnings

Bank net income is the difference between revenues and expenses, taking into account various gains, losses, and taxes. Bank revenues come from interest and noninterest sources. As expected, interest income from loans and investments makes up most of bank revenues. However, noninterest income from such things as fees, service charges, and commissions is an important and growing source of bank revenues. For example, noninterest revenues were 44 percent of total bank revenue in 2003, up from around 10 percent in the mid-1980s.

Likewise, bank expenses can be thought of as being made up of interest and noninterest components. Typically, expenses have been almost evenly divided between interest and noninterest costs. In today's low interest rate environment, however, noninterest expenses exceed interest expenses by more than 2.5 times.

Besides these revenue and expense components, bank net income is affected by other items. These include the provision for loan and lease losses, which is used to maintain the bank's allowance for loan and lease losses (ALLL), securities gains and losses, extraordinary items, and taxes.

Factors That Influence Bank Earnings

The level and quality of bank earnings depend upon a host of factors that are external and internal to the bank. External factors relate primarily to the environment in which the bank operates and pertain to conditions that are largely beyond its control. They determine the relative ease or difficulty a bank encounters in turning a profit. Included among external factors affecting bank earnings performance are laws, regulations, economic conditions, technological change, and competition.

Instances where external factors have influenced profitability are fairly easy to find. For example, in the 1980s, declines in the agriculture, energy, and commercial real estate sectors in various regions across the country contributed to high loan losses at many banks, causing earnings to plunge. In the early 1990s, the downward slide in interest rates improved margins at many banks, causing earnings to surge.

Despite the importance of external events on bank performance, some suggest that internal factors may play an even more important role. They note that "... while poor economic conditions make it more difficult to steer a profitable course, [a bank's] policies and procedures ... have the greater influence on whether [it] will succeed or fail."[15] To these commentators, internal factors can leave the bank vulnerable to outside forces. They support their view by pointing out instances where some banks in an economically distressed area fail while others in the area continue to operate profitably.

From an internal perspective, bank earnings quality depends heavily upon a number of factors. Important among these are the bank's business strategy, asset/liability mix, asset quality, and operating efficiency. As you monitor your bank's performance, keep these factors in mind and think about how they, along with external factors, have and will influence earnings performance.

Monitoring Bank Earnings[16]

Return on average assets, defined as bank net income divided by average assets (ROAA), is one of the most often used measures to judge bank performance. Table 2.9 shows the derivation of ROAA from bank revenues, expenses, and other items. By looking at the items that make up ROAA, it is possible to isolate areas that lie behind poor or deteriorating performance. From there, you can delve deeper into these areas, searching out root causes of bottom-line performance changes. Thus, the information in the table should be considered a beginning step in monitoring bank earnings performance. The following sections discuss the individual components included in the table in more detail, suggesting additional matters to consider as you review your bank's performance.

Interest income

Interest income consists of revenues from earning assets adjusted for tax benefits on tax-exempt loans, leases, and municipal securities. This revenue component is influenced by a number of factors. Some of the more important of these are a bank's business strategy (Box 2.3), the interest rate environment in which the bank operates, the proportion of earning assets on its balance sheet, and the distribution of its asset holdings. Consequently, if you see an adverse trend in your bank's interest income, look to see if the bank has changed the character of its business (for example, changed its loan mix) or if national and local interest rates have fallen. Look to see if competition in the bank's market has intensified, putting pressure on loan rates. Also, determine if nonearning assets, such as premises, real estate taken in foreclosure, or nonaccrual loans, have increased, causing interest income to fall. Look to see if the bank is changing its asset mix: for

Table 2.9

EARNINGS ANALYSIS

> Compare current period actual results with historical values. If unfavorable trends exist, ask for explanations.

| Current period | | | | Historical | |
Actual	Budget	Peer	Measure	Previous	Same period last year
			Interest income (TE)*/ average assets		
			Interest expense/ average assets		
			Net interest income/ average assets		
			Noninterest income/ average assets		
			Provision for loan loss/ average assets		
			Net income before gains, losses, and taxes (TE)/ average assets		
			Realized gains/losses on HTM and AFS securities/ average assets**		
			Taxes and extraordinary items/average assets		
			Net income/ average assets		

> Compare actual results with budget and peer to see if bank is performing according to plan and in line with similar types of banks.

*Because interest income on some bank assets may be tax free, (for example, municipal bonds), interest income from these assets is restated to a tax equivalent amount. This is done to improve the comparability of reported income among banks.

**HTM means held-to-maturity; AFS means available-for-sale.

Box 2.3

THE EFFECT OF BUSINESS STRATEGY ON NET INCOME PERFORMANCE

Business strategy can have a significant effect on all revenue and expense items for a bank. The table below gives an example of this. It provides a comparison of national averages for banks with different lending emphasis—business or consumer loans—and shows how customer orientation can have significant effects on revenues and expenses. Some possible reasons for these differences include the need for consumer banks to operate more branches to be convenient to customers. Also, consumer banks require greater staffing to serve the greater number of customers they see on a daily basis and to administer the larger volume, but smaller dollar amount, of deposit accounts and loans they handle. Invariably, these and other factors specific to customers served influence revenues and expenses and account for the differences shown in the table.

Revenues and Expenses of All U.S. Banks for 2003:
By Loan Emphasis—Business and Consumer Loans

Income/expense performance measure*	Business-oriented **banks**	Consumer-oriented ***banks***
Interest income	3.55	5.34
Interest expense	1.17	1.49
Net interest income	2.38	3.85
+Noninterest income	3.20	3.11
-Provision for loan and lease losses	.39	.96
-Noninterest expense	3.63	3.96
Net income before taxes and other items	1.56	2.04
+Securities gains and (losses)	.05	.06
-Taxes plus extraordinary items	.53	.62
Net income	1.10	1.48

*All performance measures are divided by average assets.
**Banks whose largest loan category is loans to businesses.
***Banks whose largest loan category is loans to individuals. Excludes banks with emphasis in credit card lending.

example, moving from higher-yielding assets, such as loans, to lower-yielding assets, such as securities.

Interest expense

Interest expense consists of interest payments made by the bank on deposits and other borrowings. This expense item depends heavily upon the interest rate environment the bank faces and the strategy management follows to fund bank assets.[17] As a consequence, if this ratio shows an upward trend, look to see if national/market deposit interest rates have moved. Also, check to see if management has changed the way bank assets are funded. For example, has the bank moved away from using low-cost core deposits (for example, demand and savings deposits) to using higher-cost large CDs ($100,000 or more), brokered deposits, and other borrowings to fund bank assets?

Net interest margin

Net interest margin (NIM) is the difference between interest income and interest expense. It represents the spread or gross margin on the bank's loans and investments. Beyond the factors discussed previously that can influence bank interest income and expense, the size of this spread depends upon the relative responsiveness of rates received and paid on a bank's assets and liabilities to changes in market interest rates. Among the tools banks use to help gauge the possible effects of interest rate movements on NIM are "gap analysis" and earnings at risk simulation models. These tools for judging a bank's interest rate exposure and other aspects of market risk will be discussed later in the Sensitivity to Market Risk section.

Noninterest income

This revenue component consists of such things as fees, service charges, and commissions. Like other revenue and expense components, it also depends upon such factors as the bank's business strategy and the market conditions in which the bank operates. For example, a decline in this item may indicate a shift away from activities that produce noninterest income. Bank management may have decided that certain fee-generating activities are not profitable given competition in the market or that they entail too much risk for the bank relative to income generated.

Provision for loan and lease losses

As noted in the section on asset quality, the provision for loan and lease losses is the amount set aside by a bank to maintain the ALLL at a level sufficient to absorb estimated loan losses. Whether or not a high or low value for this item is appropriate depends upon a bank's asset quality. If loan volume is growing, loan losses and nonperforming loans are increasing, and the ALLL balance is declining or estimated losses in the portfolio exceed the bank's existing ALLL balance, then a high provision for loan and lease losses may be necessary. On the other hand, if loan growth and losses are low, nonperforming loans are small and declining, and the bank's ALLL methodology indicates that the existing loan loss reserve balance appears adequate to absorb probable loan losses, a low loan loss provision may be appropriate.

Noninterest expenses

Noninterest expenses consist of salaries, depreciation, management fees, losses on asset sales, legal fees, and other overhead of the bank. Many of these expenses are affected by the operational efficiency or cost-effectiveness of the bank in providing deposits, loans, and other services to its customers. They may also be affected by the cost of resolving loan problems and losses from disposing of troubled assets. If you see an increasing trend in this ratio, you may want to look at individual expense items to see which have shown large increases over time. For example, if personnel costs have risen substantially over time, you may want to look at salaries paid to see if they are in line with those paid by others in the bank's market. You also may want to compare the bank's number of employees with peer banks to see if productivity has fallen.

Net realized securities gains, losses, taxes, and extraordinary items

These items consist of a potpourri of largely "one-time" gains, losses, and charges, (for example, securities gains/losses, accounting adjustments, gains/losses on sales of assets, etc.) They play a role in determining the bottom-line performance of every bank. However, they should not be relied upon as a significant or continued earnings source since they normally are not sustainable. If these items remain a significant part of your bank's earnings for long periods, you may want to review them more closely. One place to focus your review is on securities gains. It may be that your bank is selling off its high-yielding securities to record gains to boost current earnings. If it is doing this, your bank may be sacrificing long-term profitability since it may not be able to reinvest funds received except in lower rate instruments. Another concern with gains trading pertains to the source of the gains. Banks are required to segregate their securities holdings according to the purpose for which they are held—for trading, available-for-sale, and investment. These purposes determine how the securities are to be valued for financial reporting. If the bank is registering gains by selling investment securities, then it is likely that these securities are not being held for long-term investment and, as a result, may not be valued appropriately. This may cause the bank's financial statements to be misstated, exposing the bank, directors, and others to monetary penalties.

In summary, earnings quality refers to the composition, level, trend, and stability of bank earnings. For you, the director, and bank management, bank earnings quality is a financial report card. It tells how the bank has managed its risk exposure. Where risk management is good, earnings will be strong and earnings quality will be good. Where risk management is poor, the opposite will be the result. In such cases, dissecting earnings into its component parts provides insights regarding areas needing attention.

LIQUIDITY

Bank liquidity refers to the ability of a bank to quickly raise cash at a reasonable cost. Banks must have adequate liquidity in order to serve their customers and to operate efficiently. Those with adequate liquidity are able to pay creditors; meet unforeseen deposit runoffs; accommodate sudden, unexpected changes in loan demand; and fund normal loan growth without making costly balance sheet adjustments. Banks with poor liquidity may not be able to meet these funding demands and in extreme cases may be closed.[18]

Providing for a bank's liquidity needs can present many practical challenges. One reason is that funding demands may change suddenly and unexpectedly in response to economic and other events. Another reason is that liquidity sources, like the magician's coin, may be there one minute and gone the next. As a result, a liquidity position thought adequate under one set of circumstances may not be enough to support a bank's funding needs when things change.

This section reviews bank liquidity needs. It discusses bank liquidity sources, describes monitoring and planning for bank liquidity needs, and discusses ways to analyze a bank's liquidity position.

Sources of Liquidity

Banks can fund their operations in the following ways:

* Sell assets.

* Attract short-term and long-term deposit liabilities.

* Increase short-term and long-term borrowings.

* Increase capital funds.

The way a bank meets its funding needs depends upon the cost and availability of its funding options. Costs, which include losses on forced asset sales as well as higher interest charges, depend upon such matters as asset and liability maturity mix and marketability of asset holdings. Funding options available depend largely upon the bank's overall financial condition and creditworthiness.

Assets

Bank assets are storehouses of liquidity and theoretically any asset item can serve as a liquidity source. How well a particular asset serves in this capacity depends upon the length of time it takes to dispose of it and the price the asset brings when it is sold. Assets that can be sold at a moment's notice without any appreciable loss to the bank are ideal candidates for meeting unexpected liquidity demands. As a practical matter, few bank assets meet this ideal. For example, a bank could not quickly dispose of its building, furniture and fixtures, loans, and real estate to meet depositor demands for funds except at considerable loss.

In most instances, banks use their investment portfolio as a source of liquidity. Even securities, however, may have to be sold at a loss if an unexpected demand for funds should occur. Because of this, it is important that banks plan for future liquidity needs.

An important part of this planning process is designating the purpose served by the bank's securities holdings. Prior to 1993, banks held their securities either for investment or trading purposes. With the application of market value accounting to banks' balance sheets, banks were required to designate their investment securities as "held-to-maturity" securities (HTM securities) and "available-for-sale" securities (AFS securities).

HTM securities are those that a bank purchases with the intent (and it has the ability) to hold until maturity. Since the bank's intent is to hold its HTM securities until they mature, they are reported on a bank's balance sheet at amortized cost—the bank's cost adjusted for premium paid or discount received.

A bank may decide to hold investment securities as HTM securities for a variety of reasons. For example, if securities offer a high yield, the bank may decide to purchase and hold them until maturity simply because they provide a good return. If the securities are issued by state and local political subdivisions (for example, county and city government, water districts, school districts, etc.), the bank may purchase them as a gesture of community support. Besides return and community support motives, HTM securities purchases may play a role in the bank's liquidity management by being "pledged" or used as collateral against government deposits.

AFS securities are those that a bank purchases with the intent of selling if the need arises. AFS securities are reported on the bank's balance sheet at fair value, the value the bank could obtain for the securities at the time the balance sheet is prepared. Any difference between this value and the book value of a bank's AFS securities is reported as an unrecognized gain or loss and is shown as an adjustment to its reported capital position. It is important to note that the federal banking agencies currently do not explicitly take into account unrecognized losses in determining capital adequacy.[19] However, these losses can raise supervisory concerns if the liquidity position of a bank is strained and it has *large* unrecognized losses in its AFS securities. In the event the bank was forced to sell its AFS securities, in order to meet liquidity needs, previously unrecognized losses would have to be taken and this would negatively affect the bank's capital position.

AFS securities serve as an important source of liquidity for banks, and approximately 98 percent of U.S. banks' investment securities are held as AFS securities. Thus, when a bank needs cash for liquidity purposes, it sells some of its AFS securities. This raises the question, "What happens if these securities are not sufficient to meet liquidity needs and the bank must sell some HTM securities?" The answer is the bank "taints" its HTM securities portfolio, and it must reclassify all of these securities as AFS securities (see Box 2.4). The reclassified securities must be valued at their current market price and any unrecognized gains/losses taken into account in the bank's capital position, once again raising supervisory concerns if the reclassified securities have large embedded unrecognized losses within them and the bank's liquidity position is strained.

Box 2.4

FAS 115

The Financial Accounting Standards Board (Accounting Board) adopted its Statement of Financial Accounting Standards No. 115 or FAS 115, Accounting for Certain Investments in Debt and Equity Securities in May 1993. This statement, which became effective for bank financial reporting January 1, 1994, subjects banks to an element of market value accounting, by requiring them to designate investment securities held for liquidity purposes as AFS securities. Because these securities can be sold at any time to meet liquidity needs, banks must report them on their balance sheets at fair or market value. Remaining investment securities, HTM securities, continue to be reported at amortized cost.

With the exception of seven circumstances set out in FAS 115, no HTM security can be sold prior to maturity without "tainting" the entire HTM securities portfolio. This means that all HTM securities must be reported at their fair value and reported capital adjusted for any gain or loss from cost even if only a single issue is sold out of many. Because of this, it is important that banks carefully consider their liquidity needs before designating securities as held-to-maturity. The seven circumstances are as follows:

- Deterioration in the issuer's creditworthiness.

- Changes in tax law that eliminate or reduce the tax-exempt status of interest paid on the issuer's debt securities.

- Major business combination or asset sale that requires transfer of held-to-maturity securities to maintain the bank's existing interest rate risk position or credit risk policy.

Box 2.4 *(continued)*

- Regulatory changes that modify the permissibility or the maximum level of investment in a specific security.

- Changes in regulatory capital requirements that cause a bank to downsize by selling held-to-maturity securities.

- Significant increase in risk weights applied to debt securities for risk-based capital purposes.

- Unanticipated, isolated, nonrecurring, and unusual events that may cause the bank to sell held-to-maturity securities.

The seven circumstances are events largely out of the control of bank management. It is important to note that selling HTM securities to meet the liquidity needs of a bank is not considered an "unanticipated, isolated, nonrecurring, and unusual" event—the last item on the list. Bank management is to plan for the bank's liquidity needs.

Liabilities

A bank also can meet its funding needs through liability management. Deposits are the most important funding source for a great majority of banks and generally are their lowest-cost funding source. Chart 2.3 data show that smaller banks tend to rely more heavily on deposits to fund their assets than larger banks. However, as the decline in the deposits-to-assets ratio for both bank size groups indicates, deposit growth has not kept pace with asset growth. Furthermore, deposits are becoming increasingly more expensive as competitive alternatives available to consumers make low-cost core deposits (demand, money market, NOW, time, and savings accounts, and small denomination certificates of deposits) more scarce, forcing banks to rely more heavily on higher cost noncore deposits (large denomination CDs, brokered deposits, etc.).

Chart 2.3

DEPOSITS TO ASSETS ALL U.S. BANKS: SMALL AND LARGE BANKS

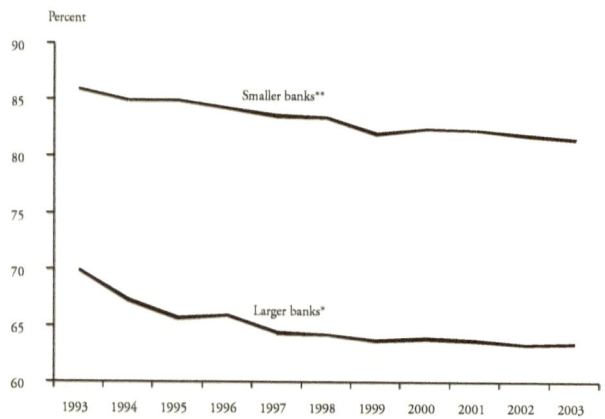

*Larger banks are those with total assets greater than $1 billion.
**Smaller banks are those with total assets less than $1 billion.
Source: Reports of Condition and Income

The scarcity of deposits has caused banks to make greater use of nondeposit liabilities to support asset growth. Two important nondeposit sources of funds are federal funds purchased (fed funds purchased) and Federal Home Loan Bank (FHLB) advances.

Federal funds are reserves held in a bank's account with its Federal Reserve Bank. If a bank has more reserves in its account than is required by the Federal Reserve, it can loan these excess reserves to other depository institutions. When a bank borrows federal funds, they are fed funds purchased. Most fed funds transactions are done on an overnight basis. However, longer-term arrangements can be made. For example, there are term fed funds that generally mature between two days and one year. Typically, fed funds purchased are viewed as a short-term funding source.

A longer-term funding source is FHLB borrowings. A bank can be an FHLB member and, if it qualifies, make use of a regional FHLB's lending programs.[20] These programs have a wide range of maturities and interest rate terms and can be used to fund residential loans and, in the case of smaller banks, fund small business, small farm, and small agribusiness loans. Because of their flexibility, banks increasingly use these loan programs as a funding source. Chart 2.4 shows how rapid this growth has been, both in number of banks borrowing at FHLBs and in the amount they have borrowed. At year-end 2003, about 77 percent of U.S. banks were FHLB members. Approximately 54 percent of these banks had loans with FHLBs, and these loans supported about 6.5 percent of total U.S. banking assets. The Gramm-Leach-Bliley Act lessened restrictions on FHLB membership for small banks and increased the types of collateral that FHLBs can accept on long-term advances.[21] As a result, FHLB advances are likely to remain a more important funding source for small community banks.

An important issue in using the liability side of the balance sheet as a liquidity management tool is the stability of a bank's liabilities. Often, fed funds, noncore deposits, and FHLB advances are available only as long as a bank is willing and able to pay for their use. Furthermore, a bank's access to these funds may be limited if its creditworthiness comes under

Chart 2.4

FHLB BANK MEMBERS AND ADVANCES OUTSTANDING

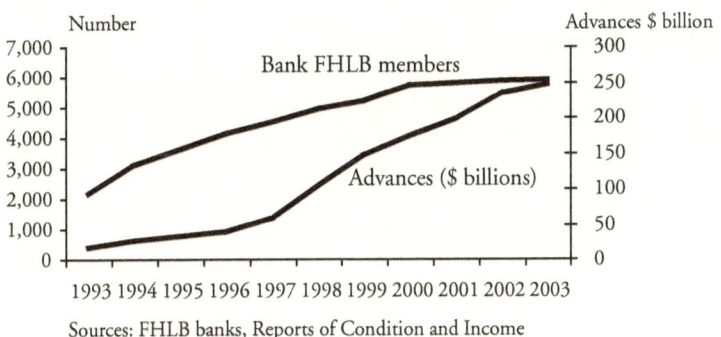

Sources: FHLB banks, Reports of Condition and Income

question or its capital slips below satisfactory levels. Because of this, banks that rely heavily on noncore deposits and nondeposit liabilities may be particularly vulnerable to liquidity pressure in times of trouble.

Until the passage of the Federal Deposit Insurance Corporation Improvement Act of 1991 (FDICIA), the liability side of the balance sheet, especially deposits, was an almost limitless funding source for a bank. As long as it was willing to pay above market rates, a bank could attract deposits. FDICIA, however, changed this by instilling greater depositor discipline over banks and by tying the use of purchased funds to bank capital.

FDICIA increased depositor discipline by making it illegal for the FDIC to take any action that would increase insurance fund losses by protecting depositors for more than the insured portion of their deposits. Because depositors risk losing all or part of the uninsured portion of their deposits, they will be less apt to keep large uninsured amounts at banks unless they are in good financial health. As a result, banks in poor or deteriorating condition may find it more difficult to retain uninsured deposits to fund their operations and thus may be more prone to liquidity problems.

FDICIA also made it more difficult for problem banks to use purchased money as a funding source. Under the law and implementing regulations, *well-capitalized* banks (refer to Table 2.3 on page 33) for capital definitions) that are not in troubled condition face no restrictions on their use of brokered deposits. However, *adequately* capitalized banks cannot accept, renew, or roll over brokered deposits unless they have a waiver from the FDIC permitting them to do so. Furthermore, they cannot pay deposit rates significantly above (75 basis points) prevailing rates in pertinent markets. *Undercapitalized* banks cannot continue their use of brokered deposits. Because of these restrictions, undercapitalized banks have fewer liability options to address liquidity needs.

FDICIA also altered the availability of the Federal Reserve's discount window to meet funding needs. Discount window advances are available to banks and other insured depository institutions to meet liquidity needs that may arise from such things as unexpectedly large withdrawals of deposits, seasonal fluctuation in deposits and loans, or exceptional circumstances. Under FDICIA, the Federal Reserve is limited on how long it may lend to undercapitalized banks without incurring any liability.[22] Additionally, FDICIA made the Federal Reserve liable for any increased loss to the FDIC insurance fund resulting from any outstanding loans to banks five days after they have become critically undercapitalized. Consequently, some banks may find discount window borrowing a more limited funding source.

Capital

A bank may use sales of new equity and debt capital instruments to help meet its funding needs. However, because raising capital requires considerable planning and can be both time consuming (securities registration requirements) and costly (underwriting charges), banks seldom use capital sales as a short-term funding source. Instead, these sales play a more important role in restoring capital and reopening other funding sources to banks.

In summary, banks have a variety of balance sheet resources to draw upon to meet expected and unexpected funding needs. However, because of law and regulatory changes, some sources of liquidity may not be as readily available as they once were. Moreover, in times of trouble, some funding avenues simply may not be open. As a result, it is essential that you and other board members establish policies that address how your bank will provide for adequate liquidity. You also must monitor the bank's liquidity position and, with management, develop plans to meet expected and unexpected funding needs.

Establishing Policies

It is important that bank policies take into account liquidity needs. For example, the investment policy should define how the bank's liquidity requirements are considered in determining the type and maturity of securities purchased. The asset/liability management policy should spell out asset and liability mix and maturity and set operating limits (for example, maximum loans-to-total deposits ratio, that helps preserve the bank's funding options).

Monitoring and Planning for Bank Liquidity

Ratio analysis

Table 2.10 presents some liquidity measures and offers thoughts on matters to consider in reviewing your bank's liquidity. The ratios included in the table, however, focus primarily on the bank's current liquidity position. It also is important to have a picture of your bank's future liquidity needs to help plan for these needs. Knowing in advance when liquidity pressure points might occur makes it possible to explore alternative ways to deal with them in advance. This advanced planning permits a more reasoned, less frantic, and less costly approach to raising funds to meet the bank's liquidity requirements. Two useful tools for looking at your bank's future liquidity position are the liquidity gap and the liquidity forecast.

Liquidity gap analysis

Liquidity gap analysis provides a picture of your bank's future funding needs by comparing the amount of assets and liabilities maturing over time. This comparison permits pinpointing large maturity mismatches that may place liquidity strains on the bank. Table 2.11 presents a sample liquidity gap calculation.

Liquidity forecasts

Liquidity forecasts identify possible future events, project how they might affect a bank's funding needs, and indicate how these needs might be met. For example, a forecast could show planned asset growth and present ways this growth may be funded. Or, it might attempt to identify future fund inflows and set out ways to re-deploy these funds to maximize the bank's earnings while providing for its liquidity needs. These ideas are illustrated in Table 2.12.

Table 2.10

RATIO ANALYSIS—LIQUIDITY

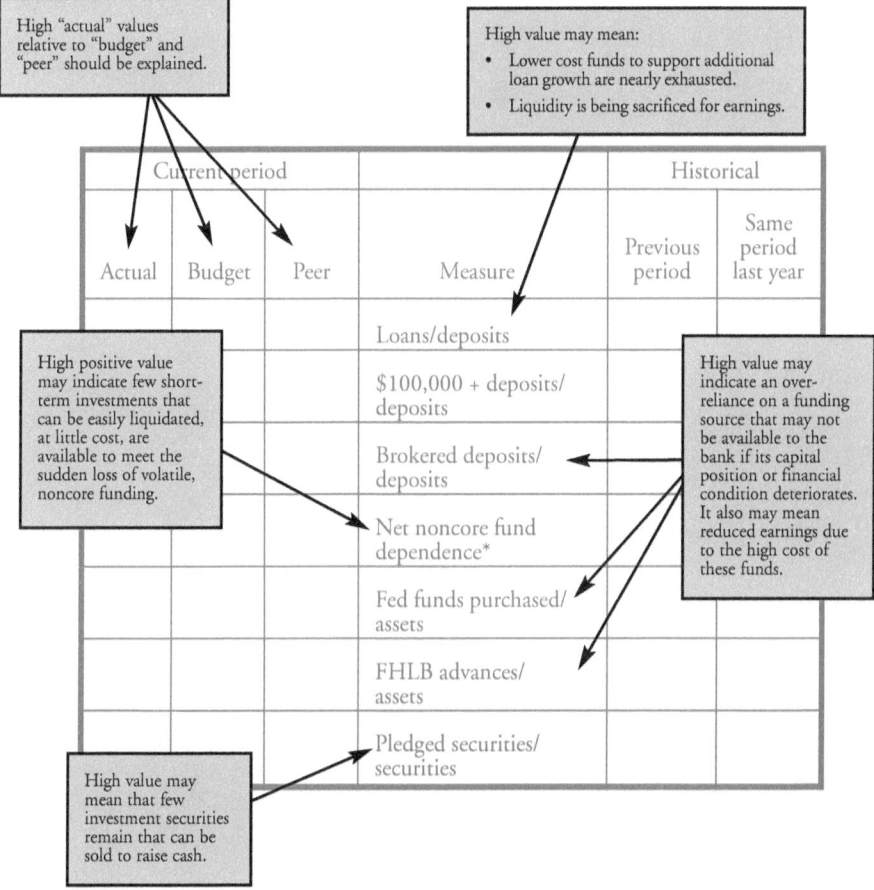

High "actual" values relative to "budget" and "peer" should be explained.

High value may mean:
- Lower cost funds to support additional loan growth are nearly exhausted.
- Liquidity is being sacrificed for earnings.

| | Current period | | | Historical | |
Actual	Budget	Peer	Measure	Previous period	Same period last year
			Loans/deposits		
			$100,000 + deposits/ deposits		
			Brokered deposits/ deposits		
			Net noncore fund dependence*		
			Fed funds purchased/ assets		
			FHLB advances/ assets		
			Pledged securities/ securities		

High positive value may indicate few short-term investments that can be easily liquidated, at little cost, are available to meet the sudden loss of volatile, noncore funding.

High value may indicate an over-reliance on a funding source that may not be available to the bank if its capital position or financial condition deteriorates. It also may mean reduced earnings due to the high cost of these funds.

High value may mean that few investment securities remain that can be sold to raise cash.

*Net noncore dependence = $\dfrac{\textit{noncore liabilities less short-term investments}}{\textit{long-term investments}}$

Shows a bank's ability to fund the loss of noncore liabilities. For large banks that rely more heavily on non-core funding, this ratio is typically positive. For community banks that rely more heavily on core deposits, this ratio often will be negative. See pages III-58, 59 of *A User's Guide for the Uniform Bank Performance Report*, March 2004, for a description of the balance sheet items that make up this ratio.

Table 2.11

SAMPLE LIQUIDITY GAP CALCULATION*

Avoid large maturity mismatches between assets and liabilities. Large negative mismatches may mean the bank is poorly positioned to meet unexpected funding needs without incurring significant cost.

	Maturity period				
	0–90 days	91–180 days	181–365 days	1–5 years	Over 5 years
Assets	25	15	20	15	25
Liabilities	40	25	15	10	10
Liquidity gap	(15)	(10)	5	5	15
Cumulative liquidity gap	(15)	(25)	(20)	(15)	0

*Values in table are in $ millions.

Examine trends in the bank's cumulative gap position to spot growing mismatches between assets and liabilities over time.

Table 2.12

LIQUIDITY FORECAST

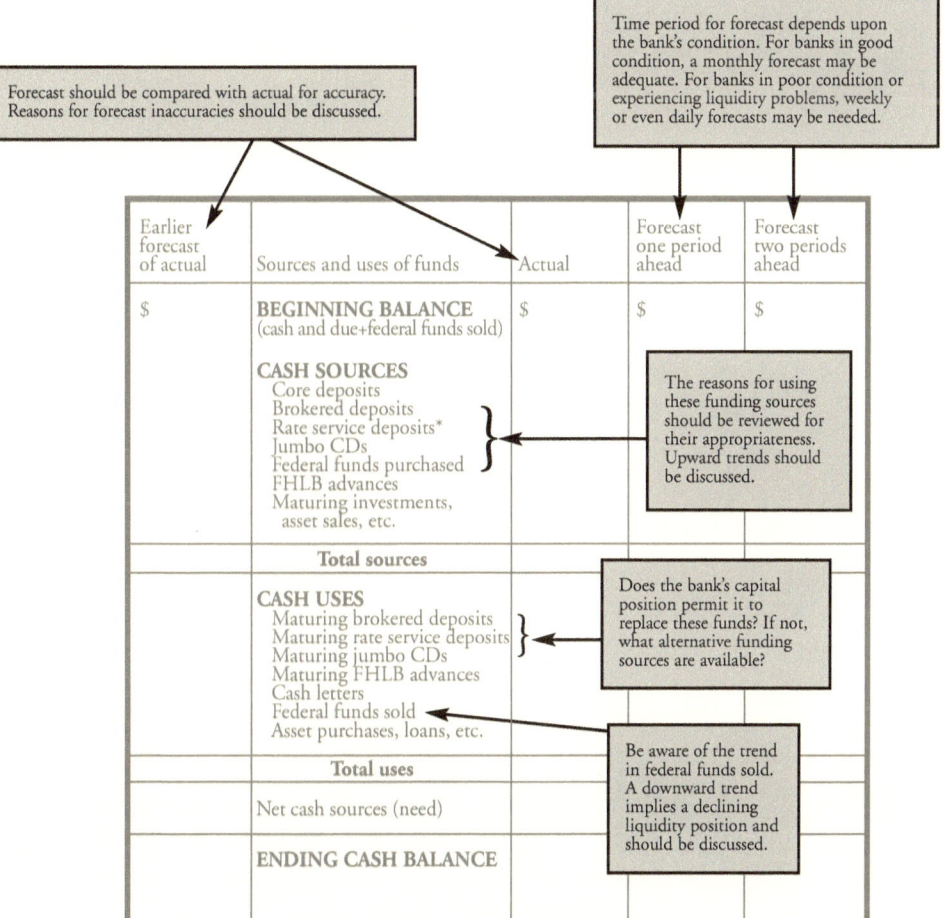

Time period for forecast depends upon the bank's condition. For banks in good condition, a monthly forecast may be adequate. For banks in poor condition or experiencing liquidity problems, weekly or even daily forecasts may be needed.

Forecast should be compared with actual for accuracy. Reasons for forecast inaccuracies should be discussed.

Earlier forecast of actual	Sources and uses of funds	Actual	Forecast one period ahead	Forecast two periods ahead
$	**BEGINNING BALANCE** (cash and due+federal funds sold)	$	$	$
	CASH SOURCES Core deposits Brokered deposits Rate service deposits* Jumbo CDs Federal funds purchased FHLB advances Maturing investments, asset sales, etc.			
	Total sources			
	CASH USES Maturing brokered deposits Maturing rate service deposits Maturing jumbo CDs Maturing FHLB advances Cash letters Federal funds sold Asset purchases, loans, etc.			
	Total uses			
	Net cash sources (need)			
	ENDING CASH BALANCE			

The reasons for using these funding sources should be reviewed for their appropriateness. Upward trends should be discussed.

Does the bank's capital position permit it to replace these funds? If not, what alternative funding sources are available?

Be aware of the trend in federal funds sold. A downward trend implies a declining liquidity position and should be discussed.

*Rate listing services list financial institutions and the rates they pay for different types of deposits. Banks use these services to publicize their rates in order to attract deposits. Large depositors use them to find institutions paying the highest deposit rates to increase their returns. Thus, rate listing services act as an information source that facilitates bringing depositors and banks together.

In conclusion, a bank's liquidity position can change quickly, and directors are responsible for ensuring that their banks can effectively deal with these changes. This requires establishing policies that address the bank's liquidity needs, monitoring its liquidity position, and planning for its future funding needs.

SENSITIVITY TO MARKET RISK

Sensitivity to market risk refers to the risk to a financial institution's earnings or capital position resulting from changes in market rates or prices, such as interest rates, equity prices, commodity prices, or foreign exchange rates. For some large institutions, foreign operations can be a significant source of market risk. Trading activities, where the institution buys and sells for its own account hoping to profit on price movements, also can be a significant source of market risk for some. For most institutions, however, the primary source of market risk stems from interest rate changes and their effects on bank earnings and capital. It is this aspect of market risk that is the focus here.

Banks are large holders of financial assets. Because of this, interest rate movements can have significant effects on their financial condition and operating performance. For example, in 1994 when market interest rates rose after a long period of decline, many banks experienced significant market value declines in their securities portfolios. Collectively, all banks nationwide recorded unrecognized losses on their available-for-sale securities (AFS securities) of $7.8 billion. This amounted to about 2.5 percent of their year-end 1994 equity capital. When rates rose again in late 1999 and into 2000, unrealized losses on AFS securities amounted to a little more than $14.1 billion, about 3.2 percent of midyear equity capital for all U.S. banks.

It is tempting to think that these unrecognized losses are unimportant. After all, they don't have an impact unless securities holdings with losses have to be sold and the losses taken. However, unrecognized losses do matter. They indicate that bank assets are not earning current market returns and that earnings would be higher if the bank could invest its assets at higher market rates. For banks with publicly traded stock, the lost earnings translate into lower stock prices as investors are less willing to purchase stock in banks with losses. Furthermore, the losses present a potential liquidity issue if securities must be sold to meet cash needs. Finally, the losses can present a capital adequacy issue if they are sufficiently large to trigger bank examiner concerns regarding the bank's safety and soundness.

As part of the bank's management team, you are responsible for understanding the nature and the level of your bank's interest rate risk-taking and how the bank's risk-taking fits into its overall business strategy. You also are responsible for ensuring that the necessary processes are in place to identify, measure, monitor, and control your bank's interest rate exposure. How detailed and formal you make these processes depends upon the size, complexity, and risk profile of your bank.

This section reviews your bank's exposure to interest rate changes. It discusses how interest rate changes can affect bank earnings and capital and the need to establish controls over a bank's interest rate risk-taking. Additionally, it describes tools to monitor bank interest rate exposure and discusses matters to consider when reviewing output from these tools. Finally, it briefly discusses using model results to assess and address the bank's interest rate risk exposure.

Interest Rate Changes and Their Effects on Earnings and Equity

Interest rate risk is composed of four components or sub-risks: repricing risk, basis risk, yield curve risk, and options risk.

Repricing risk—the risk that arises from timing differences or mismatches in rate changes or in the maturity of a bank's assets and liabilities (for example, a long-term, fixed-rate asset funded with a short-term deposit). In this example, interest income from the asset remains fixed over its life while the interest expense to fund the asset changes each time the deposit is renewed. Because interest income is fixed and interest expense can move with market rate changes, net interest income and underlying economic values increase or decrease in response to market rates. This risk according to one estimate accounts for 40-45 percent of an average bank's interest rate risk.[23]

Basis risk—the risk that changes in market interest rates may have different effects on rates received or paid on instruments with similar repricing characteristics (for example, a variable rate loan whose rate is based on the three-month Treasury bill rate that is funded with three-month certificates of deposit). Because both instruments have a similar repricing interval, there is no repricing risk. History shows, however, that deposit rates and Treasury bill rates may not identically track market rate changes. To the extent the rates do not move in tandem, there are effects to net interest income and underlying economic values. One estimate places this risk at approximately 20-45 percent of banks' interest rate risk.[24]

Yield curve risk (another form of repricing risk)—the risk that changes in market interest rates may have different effects on yields or prices on similar instruments with dissimilar repricing characteristics (for example, a change in market interest rates may affect yield on a three-month Treasury bill more or less than on a one-year Treasury bill). This can accentuate or attenuate the effects of rate change on maturity mismatches. Like other forms of repricing risk, this risk exposes a bank's net interest income and underlying economic value to changes in market rates. In terms of relative importance, one source places this risk at 5-10 percent of an average bank's interest rate risk.[25]

Options risk—the risk that arises from embedded options in a bank's assets and liabilities (for example, provisions in agreements that allow loan customers to prepay their loans or allow deposit holders to withdraw their funds early with little or no penalty). These options, if exercised, can once again affect net interest income and underlying economic values. One estimate places this risk at 10-25 percent of the interest rate risk in the average bank.[26]

In summary, these risks can affect a bank's income and value. Because of this, it is important that your board and the bank's senior management establish policies and procedures to control the bank's interest rate risk exposure and that you put in place monitoring and reporting systems to let you track compliance with established limits.

Asset-Liability Management Policy

At many banks today, the asset-liability management (ALM) policy is the primary tool for controlling interest rate risk. Although ALM policies vary from bank to bank based on individual need, most policies establish risk limits and specify lines of authority for managing interest rate risk. They set out procedures, documentation requirements, and analyses to be done prior to acquiring specified instruments and for managing the bank's investments. They indicate appropriate methods for controlling the bank's aggregate interest rate exposure. Additionally, they specify reports required by the board to monitor the bank's interest rate risk exposure, and outline the frequency these reports are provided to the board for its review of the bank's risk position. They also establish the process for handling policy exceptions, establish time frames for the board's review of the ALM policy for its adequacy and currency, and set out audit requirements for the bank's ALM function.

Monitoring bank interest rate risk

Once the board has established interest rate risk boundaries for the bank, it is important that appropriate risk measurement systems be put in place to monitor policy compliance. As previously noted, interest rate changes present risk to both bank earnings and capital. Because of this, the federal banking agencies encourage banks to put in place systems capable of measuring earnings and capital at risk.

Typically, banks use models to assess their earnings and capital exposure to interest rate changes. These models combine bank financial data, interest rate assumptions, behavioral assumptions for the bank and its customers, and finance concepts to judge a bank's potential interest rate exposures.

In general, models can be grouped into two broad categories based on the focus of the risk analysis they provide. Earnings at risk (EAR) models focus on possible changes in a bank's net interest income, noninterest income, and bottom-line profitability from interest rate movements. This risk assessment approach is sometimes referred to as a "short-term view," "accounting approach," or "earnings perspective" to judging interest rate risk. Capital at risk or economic value of equity (EVE) models, the second category of models, focus on possible changes in the market value of a bank's assets, liabilities, and off-balance sheet items due to interest rate movements and the impact these changes have on the bank's equity capital position. This approach is sometimes referred to as a "long-term view" or an "economic approach" for determining interest rate risk. As the designations "short-term" and "long-term" denote, both should be used to obtain a complete picture of a bank's interest rate risk exposure.

EAR models

Banks may develop their own EAR models or purchase models developed by others. The models they use vary with respect to their features and to what they will allow you to include, assume, and change in the model. Two EAR models commonly used by banks are gap analysis and income simulation.

Gap analysis

Gap analysis was one of the first analytical methods developed to assess banks' interest rate exposure. Because of this, it is one of the most frequently used methods by banks—for example, one 2004 survey of community banks showed that approximately 60 percent of banks responding to the survey used gap as one of their interest rate risk assessment tools.[27]

Gap analysis looks at timing differences between the repricing of interest rates on a bank's assets and liabilities to determine its interest rate exposure, making it a good tool for judging repricing risk. When these timing differences are large, the bank faces greater net income exposure than when these differences are small (see Box 2.5).

Income simulation

Income simulations are generally computer-based models that use information on a bank's current balance sheet position and assumptions about future interest rate movements, management strategies, customer behavior, and new business and reinvestment plans to project future cash flows, income, and expenses. These projections or simulations can be run for a variety of interest rate scenarios and can be used to perform "what if" analyses on the effects of interest rate changes under alternative business strategies. Many times, however, analyses are done for a base case scenario—the bank under no interest

GAP AND NET INTEREST INCOME EXPOSURE TO CHANGING INTEREST RATES

Gap analysis is one tool used by a bank to determine the possible effects of interest rate movements on net interest income and profitability. The table below presents a sample gap calculation for two banks and shows how a bank's gap position can influence its earnings. Normally, a gap report shows a bank's interest-bearing assets and liabilities according to when they reprice—the period when the interest rate received or paid on them can change.

To simplify the analysis here, repricing intervals are limited to 12 months, and interest-bearing assets and liabilities are grouped and shown as totals rather than being shown individually. After the totals, interval gaps are presented. These are calculated by subtracting total rate-sensitive liabilities from rate-sensitive assets for each bucket. The cumulative gap, the next item, is the sum of the interval gaps across the buckets. The last item, RSA/RSL, is a summary measure to give the reader some perspective on the bank's interest rate exposure. It is calculated using cumulative rate-sensitive assets and liabilities across the repricing intervals. Most banks try to keep this ratio close to 1.0, implying a neutral interest rate risk position—interest income and interest expense move by the same amount, leaving net interest income unchanged.

BANK 1 ($MILLIONS)

Measure	0–30 days	31–60 days	61–90 days	4–6 months	6–12 months
				Repricing intervals	
Total rate-sensitive assets	$5	$10	$5	$4	$16
Total rate-sensitive liabilities	$10	$20	$10	$10	$10
Interval gap	$(5)	$(10)	$(5)	$(6)	$6
Cumulative gap	$(5)	$(15)	$(20)	$(26)	$(20)
RSA/RSL	.50	.50	.50	.48	.67

Box 2.5 *(continued)*

BANK 2 ($MILLIONS)	Repricing intervals				
Measure	0–30 days	31–60 days	61–90 days	4–6 months	6–12 months
Total rate-sensitive assets	$10	$15	$20	$5	$10
Total rate-sensitive liabilities	$5	$10	$5	$4	$16
Interval gap	$5	$5	$15	$1	$(6)
Cumulative gap	$5	$10	$25	$26	$20
RSA/RSL	2.00	1.67	2.25	2.63	1.50

At one year, the focus of many gap analyses, Bank 1 is negatively gapped by $20 million—rate-sensitive liabilities exceed rate-sensitive assets by $20 million. Bank 2 is positively gapped at one year—rate-sensitive assets exceed rate-sensitive liabilities by $20 million.

If market interest rates rise by 200 basis points (2 percent) from 5 to 7 percent, interest expense for Bank 1 will rise faster than interest income causing its net interest income to fall. Using simplifying assumptions, the amount of this fall would be $400,000 (.02 x $20 million). If it is assumed that the bank's net interest income was originally $1.2 million, net interest income would decline 33 percent to $800,000. The effect on Bank 2 would be just the opposite. If the bank originally had net interest income of $1.2 million, its net interest income would rise by $400,000 to $1.6 million, an increase of 33 percent.

As this example shows, a bank's gap position tells you how interest rate changes may affect its net interest income—a negatively gapped bank is hurt by market interest rate increases, a positively gapped bank is helped. Conversely, a negatively gapped bank is helped by a rate fall; a positively gapped bank is hurt. Thus, a bank's gap position provides information on the vulnerability of its net interest income to interest rate changes.

rate change—and for rising and falling rate scenarios. In some instances, other scenarios may be presented (for example, a most likely rate change scenario).

Model results often are presented to the boards of directors and senior management in summary tables and graphs in time frames spelled out by the ALM policy. Table 2.13 presents one type of summary report you might see. In the report, the effects of a 200 basis point increase and decrease in interest rates on net interest income is compared with a no change, base case. Columns 2, 3, and 4 show how much net interest income changes under the different rate scenarios.

Table 2.13

EARNINGS AT RISK SIMULATION

| Period | Net interest income change with interest rates | | |
	No rate change (2)	Up 200 basis points (3)	Down 200 basis points (4)
Quarter 1	$400	$(20)	$20
Quarter 2	$200	$(20)	$20
Quarter 3	$500	$(80)	$100
Quarter 4	$600	$(90)	$120
Total	$1,700	$(210)	$260

Similar reports may be developed to show how net interest income may be affected under alternative business strategies for a variety of interest rate scenarios. The number of reports that can be generated is limited only by the creativity of those running the model.

To avoid information overload, you and other board members, along with senior management, should decide on scenarios that will help you best judge the bank's interest rate risk profile. In this regard, the federal banking agencies suggest:

> *Bank management should ensure that risk is measured over a probable range of potential interest rate changes, including meaningful stress situations. In developing appropriate rate scenarios, bank management should consider a*

variety of factors such as the shape and level of the current structure of interest rates and historical movements. The scenarios used should incorporate a sufficiently wide change in interest rates (for example, +/- 200 basis points over a one-year horizon) and include immediate or gradual changes in interest rates as well as changes in the shape of the yield curve in order to capture the material effects of any explicit or embedded options.[28]

The agencies also suggest that reports you receive from simulation analyses, like all reports, should be clear, concise, timely, and provide the information needed to make decisions regarding your bank's interest rate risk exposure. Reports you receive should allow you to:

- Evaluate the level and trend of the bank's aggregate risk exposure.

- Evaluate the sensitivity and reasonableness of key assumptions—such as those dealing with changes in the shape of the yield curve or in the pace of anticipated loan payments or deposit withdrawals.

- Verify compliance with the board's risk tolerance levels and limits and identify policy exceptions.

- Determine whether the bank holds sufficient capital for the level of interest rate risk being taken.[29]

Economic Value of Equity

EVE focuses on possible changes in the market value of a bank's assets, liabilities, and off-balance sheet items due to interest rate movements and the impact these changes have on the bank's equity capital position. Like EAR models, banks generally use two broad categories of models to judge their equity exposure to interest rate changes: duration analysis and economic value of equity simulation.

Duration is a time measure that can be used to assess a bank's capital exposure to small changes in interest rates. As an analytical tool, duration analysis can provide valuable insights regarding the effects of interest rate changes on the value of a bank's assets, liabilities, and hence its capital position. However, it has a number of weaknesses (for example, it is valid for only small changes in interest rates and it doesn't take into account basis risk, yield curve risk, changes in business mix, or future growth) that have caused many institutions to move to economic value of equity simulation models as a tool to judge their capital exposure to interest rate changes.

With economic value of equity analysis, an attempt is made to forecast the effects of interest rate changes on the value of a bank's capital. This is done by looking at the net effects of interest rate changes on the market value of a bank's assets and liabilities.

Unfortunately, many bank assets and liabilities are not actively traded on organized markets and, as a consequence, it is difficult to determine changes in their market values resulting from interest rate movements. As a result, market value changes are often estimated using present value analysis.

With present value, the market price of an income-producing asset or an expense-causing liability is equal to the present value of its

Table 2.14

ECONOMIC VALUE OF EQUITY SIMULATION ($THOUSANDS)

Interest rate change	Market value of equity	Percent change in market value
-200 basis points	$2,512	(18.77)
-100 basis points	$2,819	(8.87)
Base case—no change	$3,093	0
+100 basis points	$3,348	8.25
+200 basis points	$3,601	16.43

discounted cash flows over the life of the asset or liability. Therefore, by making assumptions regarding cash flows and yields, EVE models can determine the effect of interest rate changes on the market value of a bank's assets and liabilities and, hence, its capital. Like income simulations, EVE simulations draw information from a large number of sources internal and external to the bank and rely heavily on assumptions. Also like income simulations, EVE simulations can be run for a wide variety of business strategies and interest rate scenarios, and simulation results are generally presented to directors and senior management in summary form. The content and the format of these summaries depend upon what the board needs to judge the bank's risk profile. Table 2.14 presents an example of a summary report you might see.

In summary, banks use models to assess their earnings and capital vulnerability to changes in interest rates. EAR models provide a short-term perspective on a bank's net interest income and bottom-line profitability. EVE models provide a long-term view on its capital exposure. The two approaches to risk measurement complement one another and can be viewed as two sides of the interest rate risk coin.

Integrity of the interest rate risk measures: Matters to consider

Because you receive model results in summary form, you may not be aware of the many complexities associated with their use. Many times, you may treat the whole interest rate risk measurement process as a "black box." Data are input into the black box, the model, where something happens. After blinking of lights and a few whirrs, results come out. However, models make use of a lot of financial data, rely on many assumptions, and utilize innumerable finance theories to measure a bank's interest rate risk. If there were ever a process where the old computer maxim "garbage in, garbage out" is particularly apropos, it is the interest rate risk measurement process. Therefore, if you are to have confidence in the interest rate risk exposure information you are presented, it is important that you become familiar with your bank's models, the assumptions used in them, and the accuracy of their output.

Individual models have different strengths and weaknesses. Some may excel at capturing repricing risk, while others may be particularly good in assessing the risk exposure of assets with embedded and explicit options. Because of this, it is important that models used by your bank are capable of capturing the important aspects of its interest rate risk exposure. Although no one expects you to be a finance wizard or a modeling expert, it is important that you are generally familiar with the capabilities of the models your bank uses and that you are satisfied that they meet the bank's needs. Ask management or the models' vendor how they work and to discuss the strengths and weaknesses of the analyses they provide. As one expert put it, make the "black box" a "glass box." By doing so, you can gain perspective on the suitability of models used by your bank and your bank's ability, given its level of expertise, to effectively use them.

Another area that deserves your scrutiny in judging the adequacy of interest rate risk estimates is the assumptions used to generate them. Models use assumptions because of inadequate or unavailable data. Many times these assumptions can be imprecise. Yet, they can greatly influence results obtained from models. Because of this, it is important that assumptions are well documented and checked for reasonableness and consistency.

The large number of assumptions used in models makes it difficult to review them all. As a result, you may want to focus your attention on a few key assumptions, assumptions that may be driving model results. Two areas where you may want to direct your attention are the interest rate assumptions used in the model and assumptions regarding the behavior of the bank's deposits.

Interest rate assumptions are important model inputs. Many times models use a few key or "driver rates" from which all other rates are derived. With respect to these driver rates, you might want to ask yourself, "What is the direction and amount of change used?" "What are the changes in short- and long-term rates (yield curve) assumed?" "What is the source of the interest rate forecast and what is the basis for the assumed changes in rates?" "What is relationship between driver rates and other rates used in the model, and what is the basis for the assumed relationship?" "Does the rate information used in the model seem reasonable given reports in the financial press?"

Besides interest rate assumptions, another area to pay close attention is assumptions regarding the bank's deposits. Many bank deposits, such as demand deposits, savings, NOW, and MMDA (non-maturity deposits), don't have specified maturities and interest rate reset dates. This requires that many assumptions be made regarding the timing of cash flows from these products when they are input into gap and simulation models. Since deposits are some of the largest items on a bank's balance sheet, assumptions pertaining to their behavior are critical to the model's accuracy. Consequently, ask about the assumptions made about deposit behavior and the basis for them. For example, "Were studies done on deposit account behavior in response to market rate and deposit rate changes?" "Did these studies cover several interest rate cycles?" "Did they account for changes in the number and types of competitors, introduction of new deposit products, and marketing initiatives and management's actions to promote/discourage use of specific deposit products?" "Was consideration given to factors that may cause changes to historical relationships between market rate changes and the bank's deposit balances?"

Finally, it is important that you and other board members monitor your bank's interest rate risk measurement process to determine its continued adequacy. This includes ensuring that management has provided adequate training for bank personnel who run and interpret model results, has established checks on model data input to ensure accuracy, and has checked model results with actual bank performance (a process called "back testing") in order to judge model accuracy. Where deficiencies are noted, corrective plans should be developed, implemented, and tracked until completed.

In summary, models used to measure a bank's interest rate exposure can be extremely complex. Understanding these complexities is not your job. Instead, your job, after establishing policy limits, is to monitor the bank's interest rate risk position to ensure that it stays within limits set by the board. Models are valuable monitoring tools to judge your bank's interest rate risk-taking. To have confidence in the results from models used by your bank, it is important you are familiar with their limitations and weaknesses, the validity of the assumptions used in them, and their accuracy in quantifying your bank's risk exposure.

Using model results to protect the bank

Model results provide a picture of a bank's possible interest rate risk exposure. If this exposure is within policy limits set by the board, little may have to be done. On the other hand, if the bank's exposure is outside policy limits, some action may be needed to bring it back into policy compliance.

There are a variety of approaches a bank can use to mitigate its interest rate risk. Often, appropriate ways for addressing the bank's risk exposure are spelled out by the board of directors in the ALM policy. The approaches that are permitted by the board depend largely on the bank's size, complexity of its assets and liabilities, and the sophistication of its management. For instance, if the bank is smaller, it may rely on balance sheet adjustments to lessen its risk exposure. If it is asset-sensitive (more rate-sensitive assets reprice than liabilities exposing net interest income to market rate declines), the bank might seek or encourage shorter-term deposits by offering higher rates on those deposits and emphasizing the availability of short-term deposits in its marketing campaigns. On the other hand, if the bank is liability-sensitive (more of its rate-sensitive liabilities reprice faster than its assets exposing net interest income to market rate rise), it may follow an opposite strategy, discouraging short-term deposits and encouraging long-term deposits. Additionally, the bank might make adjustments in the repricing structure of its assets. Depending upon its exposure, the bank might acquire assets (make loans, buy securities, etc.) with longer or shorter-term repricing schedules.

In addition to balance sheet adjustments, a bank might use swaps, options, futures, and other off-balance sheet items to lessen its interest rate exposure. It is important to note, however, that generally only larger banks use these off-balance sheet tools to manage their interest rate risk exposure. This is because the minimum transaction size for some of these tools, such as swaps, is too large to be practical for small banks. Additionally, their effective use often requires a degree of expertise and sophistication that may not be available at many smaller banks. Regardless of size, if your bank is using or is planning to use off-balance sheet techniques to manage its interest rate risk, it is important that you are aware of any risks stemming from their use.

Additionally, it is important that you are comfortable with the skills and expertise of those charged with using these techniques. If you are uncertain about the advisability of using off-balance interest rate risk management tools and the bank's ability to effectively and safely use them, seek independent advice on their appropriateness given the nature of your bank's assets and liabilities and its internal expertise.

Once plans have been developed to address the bank's interest rate exposure, it is important that the board review the outcome of actions taken. In this review, you may want to look at management's effectiveness in implementing decisions to address the bank's interest rate risk. Also, you may want to review how effective risk control decisions were in controlling the bank's risk exposure.

In summary, your bank is a large holder of financial assets, and because of this, it can be subject to significant interest rate risk exposure. To measure this exposure, it may use models. These models can be important measurement tools and a significant part of the bank's interest rate risk management process. By being familiar with the models your bank uses and understanding the information they generate, you can be more effective in monitoring your bank's compliance with established policy limits. This familiarity also helps you understand the nature of the bank's risk-taking, aids you in posing questions to management on actions to be taken, and assists you in judging the adequacy of action to bring the bank into policy compliance if necessary.

Endnotes

[1]Since January 2, 1996, the Federal Reserve has separately rated state member banks' and bank holding companies' risk management, focusing attention on: the strength of board and senior management oversight; adequacy of policies, procedures, and limits; adequacy of risk measurement, monitoring, and management information systems; and comprehensiveness of internal controls. The rating ranges from one to five, with a one designating strong risk management and a five indicating unsatisfactory risk management. See Federal Reserve System SR 95-51 (Sup), "Rating the Adequacy of Risk Management Processes and Internal Controls of State Member Banks and Bank Holding Companies," November 15, 1995.

[2]Besides providing protection, capital levels are often used to set limits on certain bank actions such as investment in premises, loans to a single borrower, and maximum amount of dividend payout.

[3]Off-balance sheet items include such things as standby letters of credit, unfunded loan commitments, interest rate swaps, and commercial letters of credit. Prior to the introduction of risk-based capital guidelines, banks were not required to provide capital for these items because these assets were held off-balance sheet. Risk-based capital standards instituted capital requirements for these items.

[4]The Federal Deposit Insurance Corporation Improvement Act of 1991 requires that the risk-based capital standards take into account more than credit risk. For example, additional matters to be considered are interest rate risk, credit concentration risk, and nontraditional activity risk.

[5]For example, dividends may be the only income source the bank's parent bank holding company has to service its debt obligations. Without dividend income, the parent company may default on its loans, causing lenders to take control of the bank.

[6]The Uniform Bank Performance Report is a valuable source of peer information. This report is provided to your bank quarterly by its primary federal banking supervisor. It also may be accessed online from the "Reports & Statistics" section of the FDIC website, *http://www.fdic.gov/quicklinks/bankers.html*

[7]Lynn D. Seballos and James B. Thompson, "Underlying Causes of Commercial Bank Failure in the 1980s," *Economic Commentary*, (Cleveland: Federal Reserve Bank of Cleveland, September 1, 1990), p. 3. Fred C. Graham and James E. Homer, "Bank Failure: An Evaluation of the Factors Contributing to the Failure of National Banks," in *The Financial Services Industry in the Year 2000: Risk and Efficiency—Proceedings of a Conference on Bank Structure and Competition May 11-13, 1988,* (Chicago: Federal Reserve Bank of Chicago, May 1988), pp. 408-413.

[8]Credit risk is not the only matter a bank must consider in making loans. For example, increased lending may require reallocation of assets, generation of deposits, or increase in borrowing. This may have implications for the bank's asset/liability mix, liquidity, and interest rate exposure.

[9]*Commercial Bank Examination Manual,* (Washington, D.C.: Board of Governors of the Federal Reserve System, March 1994, updated through November 2004), Section 2040.1.

[10]*Interagency Policy Statement on the Allowance for Loan and Lease Losses Methodologies and Documentation for Banks and Savings Institutions,* July 2, 2001.

[11]"The paramount duty of management and of boards of directors is to the corporation's shareholders. [However,] It is in the long-term interest of the stockholders for the corporation to treat its employees well, to serve its customers well, ... and to have a reputation for civic responsibility. Thus, to manage the corporation in the long-term interest of the stockholders, management and the board of directors must take into account the interests of the corporation's other stakeholders." The Business Roundtable, *Statement on Corporate Governance*, September 1997, p. 3.

[12]The standard of care directors are to exercise in their bank oversight has been subject to controversy. This controversy seems to have been resolved with the 1997 Supreme Court decision, Atherton vs. Federal Deposit Insurance Corporation. The Court held: *State law sets the standard of conduct for officers and directors of federally insured savings institutions as long as the state standard ("such as simple negligence ") is stricter than that of §1821(k). The federal statute nonetheless sets a "gross negligence" floor, which applies as a substitute for state standards that are more relaxed.* Thus, it appears that directors who act independently, remain informed, and act with a good faith belief that their decisions are in the best interests of the bank have less fear of legal liability than before the Court's decision.

[13]Robert H. Fabian, "Some of the Legal Responsibilities of Bank Directors," *The Bank Director*, ed. Richard B. Johnson, (Dallas: SMU Press, 1974), p. 66.

[14]In some instances, even good earnings performance may be indicative of poor management practices if they are the result of sacrifices in asset quality.

[15]*Bank Failure, An Evaluation of the Factors Contributing to the Failure of National Banks*, (Washington, D.C.: Office of the Comptroller of the Currency, June 1988), p. 1.

[16]This section draws heavily on information taken from *A User's Guide for the Uniform Bank Performance Report*, (Washington, D.C.: Federal Financial Institutions Examination Council, March 2004). For an alternative presentation on earnings performance, see Section I of this guide.

[17]Bank capital also affects interest expense. Since capital is a source of funds, using it to support assets reduces interest expense. Additionally, since it acts as a source of repayment, strong capital may reduce a bank's interest cost on other borrowings.

[18]Under the Federal Deposit Insurance Act, a bank must be able "to pay its obligations or meet its depositors' demands in the normal course of business." If it cannot, the bank may be considered "liquidity insolvent," and may be turned over to a conservator or receiver. See 12 U. S.C. 1821 (c).

[19]Starting October 1, 1998, banks may include up to 45 of pretax unrealized gains on AFS equity securities in their Tier 2 capital. Since banks are generally prohibited from holding equity securities, only in rare instances would a bank have equity securities whose gains could be included in its Tier 2 capital.

[20]The Financial Institutions Reform, Recovery and Enforcement Act of 1989 (FIRREA) extended membership eligibility in the Federal Home Loan Bank system to commercial banks and credit unions. Before FIRREA, only thrifts and insurance companies could be stockholders and borrowers at a Federal Home Loan Bank.

[21]The Gramm-Leach-Bliley Act of 1999 (GLB) widened access by eliminating the requirement that a community financial institution (an insured institution with average total assets over preceding three-year period of less than $500 million) have at least 10 percent or more of its

assets in residential mortgage loans in order to be eligible for Federal Home Loan Bank membership. It also enabled community financial institutions to post small business, small farm, and small agribusiness loans as collateral for long-term advances. In addition, GLB lifted the cap on the amount of other real estate-related assets, such as commercial real estate loans, that FHLB members can post as collateral.

[22]A Federal Reserve Bank can loan to an undercapitalized but viable bank no more than 60 days in any 120-day period. This period can be extended for additional 60-day periods as long as the borrowing bank is certified as viable.

[23]Leonard M. Matz, *Self Paced Asset/Liability Training*, (Austin, Texas: 1998, Sheshunoff Information Services), pp. 1-8 and 1-9.

[24]_____, *Self Paced Asset/Liability Training*, (Austin, Texas: 1998, Sheshunoff Information Services,), pp. 1-8 and 1-9.

[25]_____, *Self Paced Asset/Liability Training*, (Austin, Texas: 1998, Sheshunoff Information Services,), pp. 1-8 and 1-9.

[26]_____, *Self Paced Asset/Liability Training*, (Austin, Texas: 1998, Sheshunoff Information Services,), pp. 1-8 and 1-9.

[27]Survey of Commercial Banks in the Tenth Federal Reserve District, February 2004, Federal Reserve Bank of Kansas City. A discussion of survey results can be found at *http://www.kansascityfed.org.*

[28]*Joint Agency Policy Statement: Interest Rate Risk*, May 1996, p. 29.

[29]*Joint Agency Policy Statement: Interest Rate Risk*, May 1996, p. 30.

Chapter 3

OTHER RESOURCES
FOR BANK DIRECTORS

This booklet highlights many matters that directors might consider in governing their banks. It includes discussions on bank supervision and regulation and points out common regulatory compliance pitfalls. Additionally, it discusses bank financial soundness, covering topics on capital, asset quality, management, earnings, liquidity, and sensitivity to market risk and suggests areas to consider in judging bank performance.

In addition to this booklet, there are other resources that you may want to consult to further your study of banking. For example, there are many education programs and publications designed to help directors better supervise their banks. Banking associations, at the national and state level, sponsor seminars and training sessions for interested directors. Additionally, these associations often have information on other training opportunities open to directors. There also are numerous publications that can help directors supplement or build their banking knowledge. A sampling of these is grouped together in the next sections.

Banking Manuals

The most definitive information on matters to consider in evaluating a bank can be found in the examination manuals used by the banking agencies. These manuals, at least those of the federal banking agencies, are available to the public and can be ordered directly from the agencies or their representatives. Additionally, they can be obtained electronically from the agencies at their Internet sites. For the Comptroller of the Currency, look under "Publications." For the Federal Reserve, look under "Banking Information and Regulation," "Supervision," "Supervision Manuals." For the FDIC, look under "Publications and Documents," "Manuals," "Manual of Examination Policies." Also on the FDIC site, there is a special area that includes information that bank directors might find useful. Look for the "Directors Corner." It is included under the "Bankers" section of the FDIC home page.

- Federal Deposit Insurance Corporation–*http://www.fdic.gov.*

- Federal Reserve System–*http://www.federalreserve.gov*

- Office of the Comptroller of the Currency–*http://www.occ.treas.gov*

It is important to note that the manuals are lengthy and discuss matters in more detail than may be typically needed by directors. However, you can make them more "user friendly" if you access them electronically and use your Internet browser to search for key words and phrases on topics in which you have an interest. Regardless of how you access them, either obtaining a hard copy or viewing them electronically, they can be invaluable reference tools in helping you understand matters that may come before the board.

Director Guides

The publications included here are less definitive but no less valuable resources for directors. Each summarizes matters of importance to bank directors, differing in the emphasis given to individual topics. For example, the first three publications are more general in their orientation, outlining director responsibilities and offering suggestions on how to meet these responsibilities. The next work follows a more specific approach, focusing on things to look for when reviewing board reports. The last work provides an overview of banking regulation and what it seeks to accomplish.

Pocket Guide for Directors: Guidelines for Financial Institutions Directors. Washington, D.C.: Federal Deposit Insurance Corporation, 1988.

The Director's Book. Washington, D.C.: Office of the Comptroller of the Currency, 1997.

The Director's Primer: A Guide to Management Oversight and Bank Regulation. 3rd ed. Atlanta: Federal Reserve Bank of Atlanta, 2002.

Detecting Red Flags in Board Reports: A Guide for Directors. Washington, D.C.: Office of the Comptroller of the Currency, 2003.

- Spong, Kenneth. *Banking Regulation: Its Purposes, Implementation, and Effects.* 5th ed. Kansas City: Federal Reserve Bank of Kansas City, 2000.

Bank Director Colleges

During the 1990s, state banking departments, often in conjunction with banking associations and state universities, established director colleges to provide outside directors with information and tools to help them in their bank oversight. Generally, directors attending these colleges meet monthly, over the course of several months, and are exposed to a wide range of regulatory and bank operating matters that may be of particular value to them in their bank oversight. Provided below is contact information for some of these colleges.

- Florida Directors College, contact the Florida Bankers Association, *http://www.floridabankers.com*

- Georgia Directors College, contact the Community Bankers Association of Georgia, *http://www.cbaofga.com*

- North Carolina Bank Directors College, contact the North Carolina Commissioner of Banks, *http://www.banking.state.nc.us*

- Oregon Bank Directors College, contact the Oregon Bankers Association & Independent Community Banks of Oregon, *http://www.oregonbankers.com*

- South Carolina Bank Directors College, contact the South Carolina Bankers Association, *http://www.scbankers.org*

- Virginia Bank Directors College, contact the Virginia State Corporation Commission, Bureau of Financial Institutions, *http://www.scc.virginia.gov*

- West Virginia Directors College, contact the West Virginia Association of Community Bankers, Inc., *http://WVacb.com*

Banking Associations

Banking associations are another important educational resource. Many provide seminars, classes, telephone conference calls, online courses, and written materials that are invaluable to bank directors and banking personnel in learning about bank operations and regulatory/ supervisory matters. Usually the associations' offerings can be found by clicking "Education" on their home page. The "Events" section is another handy place to look.

Basic Training for Bank Directors

Banking associations and consultants provide many services and programs that are of great value to outside directors. So do all supervisory agencies. One of these programs is *Basic Training for Bank Directors*. The program is a half-day, multimedia presentation based on this book where directors attend a board meeting of a fictitious bank, Insights Bank and Trust. During the meeting, the bank's officers report to the board, and these reports invariably raise questions about the bank's performance and its exposure to credit, liquidity, and market risks. The primary goal of the program is to provide outside directors with the basic tools to help them be good questioners on risk taking and the effectiveness of risk management at their banks.

Basic Training for Bank Directors is available through a number of Federal Reserve Banks. Directors wanting to take advantage of this training opportunity should check with the Reserve Bank in their District.

Insights for Bank Directors

Insights for Bank Directors is the Federal Reserve's online course for bank directors. The course is provided free at *www.stlouisfed.org /col/director*. Like its progenitor, *Basic Training for Bank Directors* on which the course is loosely based, this online course provides information on analyzing bank performance and managing credit, liquidity, and market risks that directors, especially new directors, may find useful. The course can be used as a study tool or used as a reference guide, depending upon individual need.

Other information available electronically

In addition to Internet sites for the federal banking agencies referenced previously, other sites directors may find useful are those for the Federal Financial Institutions Examination Council and the Conference of State Bank Supervisors. These sites provide a wealth of information on banking conditions and performance, regulatory pronouncements, and policy statements. Additionally, they provide gateways to other sites that may be of interest to directors.

- Conference of State Bank Supervisors—*http://www.csbs.org*

- Federal Financial Institutions Examination Council—*http://www.ffiec. gov*

A–B

C

O–P

R–S

T–Z

www.ingramcontent.com/pod-product-compliance
Lightning Source LLC
Chambersburg PA
CBHW020255290526
45784CB00003B/1264